PosiTrends or Negatrends?

Dealing Positively
with the Third Millennium

PosiTrends

or

negatrends?

Eric Butterworth

DeVorss Publications

ISBN: 0-87516-721-7
Library of Congress Catalog Card Number: 98-72264

Second Printing, 1999

DeVorss & Company, Publisher
P.O. Box 550
Marina del Rey, CA 90294

Printed in The United States of America

To Olga:

My number-one student after 50 years' teaching . . .
Who knows my philosophy better than I do . . .
Who proof-checks the validity of my Truth . . .
My partner in a regular Sunday spiritual "duet" . . .
My wife, my lover, and my best friend

Contents

PROLOGUE   *xi*

INTRODUCTION   *xv*

TRENDS   *xix*

1. The Ground of Being   *1*

2. *In*trepreneurship for Everyone   *15*

3. Managing Your Own Health Care   *29*

4. The Relationship Revolution   *41*

5. Dealing with Stress   *55*

6. The Toxic Effect of Words   *67*

7. The Word Is *Integrity*   *81*

8. A Heritage of Gentleness   *95*

9. Victory over Excessive Dependencies   *109*

10. *En*tirement in the Golden Age   *121*

11. Quo Vadis?   *137*

Prologue

We begin the book *Positrends or Negatrends?* on a note of fantasy. We are going to see the Times Square–New Year's Eve scenario as a 'rite of passage' of modern society into a new age of exciting possibilities for humankind.

The scene: New York City's Times Square

The time: Midnight of December 31st, 1999

The event: Descent of the ball of light, familiar sight of many a New Year's past . . . and *you* are there.

We have seen it all before—the great crowds, the charade of "breathless anticipation" as the countdown to midnight proceeds.

But this year it is different: the entrance into the Third Millennium. The throngs of people, come to celebrate, seem unusually restrained—or should we say *apprehensive*? For there has been a media blitz of "end-of-the-world" scenarios predicting earthquakes, mudslides, floods, and fires.

Then, as the ball of light finally touches down, there seems to be an actual sigh of relief as the revelers erupt in a happy celebration. The year 2000 has long been a metaphor for fantasies of everything from out-of-control scientific futurism to religion's end-of-the-world battle of Armageddon. (A recent poll shows that 59 percent of Americans believe that the world will eventually come to an end.)

There has been much discussion in books and on TV of the grim prophecies of Nostradamus, the 16th-century astrologer. Many viewers experienced some degree of panic as the media built on their emotions. There are reports of cases of mass hysteria based upon premillennial fears, building into sheer terror as the end of the century approaches. "Millennium Syndrome" has now joined the list of psychological complexes.

The word *prophecy* needs to be understood, along with the prophets and the act of prophesying. The prophets of the Old Testament were not fortune-tellers, looking ahead to a future that was foreordained. They were "voices crying in the wilderness," sensing that there were negative energy patterns in the collective consciousness of the race, building to a negative end. This is why they cried "Repent!" They were not saying that the world is coming to an end. Instead: "There is a dangerous trend that could lead to chaos if certain streams of consciousness remain unchanged." But the good news is: if you will change the character of your consciousness, chaos will not ensue, and it should not. Join your thoughts in altering this "negatrend"* so that the world may go steadily forward.

Listen! The clock is striking midnight. The ball of light has come to rest. It is the year 2000. It is the dawn of a new era. It is the gateway to a Golden Age in human history. Whereas the doomsayers have had their sobering awareness that life will go on, so the celebrants of a "Golden Age in human history" have had theirs too. For the New Age of spiritual power embodying their predictions will be as ephemeral as the failed Doomsday, and the 21st century will be no different from the 20th unless people on the planet are different.

In our fantasy, today and every day is January 1, 2000. The sun has risen, and life goes on as usual. It is a day like any other day, with things unfolding in your life as you expect them to; but perhaps for some few, even possibly for many—and hopefully for *you* —with things unfolding as you create them in a truly *new*, high, level of consciousness.

But that's no fantasy!

*See p. xx.

Introduction

What does the new Millennium mean? Oh yes, it *is* the inauguration of a new thousand-year period of human history. But that deals with *time*, which is a process that we have created to attempt to record the unfoldment of the eternal Now. "What does it *mean?*" is the wrong question. More relevant is the question "What *can* it mean?"

The Millennium *can* be an excellent opportunity for humankind to let go of the past and resolve to make an end to warfare and violence on the planet, to make an end to drugs and guns, to make an end to the mindless raping of the earth's ecological systems.

As we count down to the Millennium, we are identifying some of the prevailing trends of personal experience in contemporary living. They represent some of the important issues of our time. Dealing with these trends is by no means all that needs to be done to bring the Kingdom of Heaven on earth. But it is a positive step in the right direction.

We are dealing with these tendencies of society not as objectives to be resolved by the world "out there," but rather as goals on a *personal* level, on the basis of "*you* make the difference." In the end, *Positrends or Negatrends?* comes down to a simple program of personal growth. If you address it seriously, you will be taking a positive step toward becoming a fully functioning person. And you will be making a small but mighty contribution to the positive energy of the planet as we live in the Third Millennium.

We are going to view this entrance into the New Millennium as a 'rite of passage' of contemporary society into a new age of exciting discoveries for humankind. We want to fantasize the Millennium as a 'now' experience. So every day we can visualize the Times Square ball of light falling dramatically to herald the coming into our life of the Kingdom-of-God possibilities. This will give dramatic continuity to the celebration of this special New Year.

The beginning of a new year invariably sees the surfacing of many seers and psychics who purport to see into the future and who give a forecast of the year to come, a list of events that will occur, who will marry and who will divorce and who will die.

But the prophet does not see into the future. No one can do that. The future is Now! He/she is sensitive to streams of consciousness, directions that *if continued* will lead to an inevitable end. In other words: *trends. But trends may be positive or negative, and the tone may be changed.* Paul: "Be ye transformed by the renewing of your mind."

We will introduce the terms **negatrend**, identifying a negative tendency in human life, and **positrend** —a spiritual treatment for dealing with it. Included is an essay to stimulate your thought on the subject, for these words can have increasing value to you in your practice of the Truth of the New Age.

A trend is an activity, not a static thing. It suggests movement and change. Sometimes when we are facing a challenging issue, we cry out, "Where are we going?" It is a good question. Someone has said, "Look where you are going, because you will surely go where you are looking." Attention is the key to life. *You tend to become whatever you give attention to.* We grow like that which we admire, the thing that occupies our attention most of the time.

A prosperity consciousness does not spontaneously appear in one's life. It is a mental force made real by where we are looking. The medieval mystic Angelus Silesius wrote, "What thou seest, man, / That too become, thou must; / God, if thou seest God, / Dust if thou seest dust." If your attention is fixed on the reality of ever-present abundance, you will tend to attract to yourself conditions of prosperity. You will reveal a *trend* toward affluence.

Look for a repetition of experiences in your life, and instead of giving vent to paranoid thoughts ("Why is the world picking on me?") consider that you are seeing a trend in the same sense that, if you keep coming down with some virus or other, there is a *trend* involved—your mental compass is off. However, you reset your compass by focusing on conditions as you would like them to be. You then begin to see a new trend—one toward the good.

When we grasp this idea, we are like a child playing with a magnifying glass who discovers that when held to the rays of the sun, it will cause a scrap of paper to burst into flame. The child is amazed.

And *we* are amazed when we discover that passing through the lens of concentrated attention, thought becomes power.

But even with all the sunlight and the most perfect magnifying glass in the world, with no steadiness of hand, the paper will not burst into flame. And given all the thought and intellect in the world, but no fixity of purpose, no concentrated attention, a person may become a good encyclopedia of facts but will never be a creator. When we have lack and limitation in our lives, it is as foolish to blame God as it is to blame the sunlight for not setting fire to the paper when we do not hold the lens steady.

By the law of mind action, the more you focus your attention on a condition in the visible realm, the more pronounced that condition becomes. Take away the attention, and the condition tends to disappear. For instance, while driving a car that has specks on the windshield, you can center your attention on the specks of dust and dirt, or on the imperfections in the glass, and you will not be able to see through the glass. *Or* . . . you can look right *through* the glass and give your attention to the traffic beyond—and the windshield and its imperfections will tend to disappear. They are no longer a barrier to you.

For now we see in a mirror dimly, but then face to face. Now I know in part; then I shall understand fully even as I have been fully understood (1 Cor. 13:12).

Trends

Life is a changing experience that involves many "streams of consciousness." It is not a static condition that may be characterized by an "X" marking the spot in time and place where something happened. This perception of life misreads how life is lived. You do not jump from good fortune to misfortune, from illness to wholeness. Something may occur to you that shakes up your whole world. It came over you so swiftly that you "didn't know what hit you." You may say, "I don't know what happened." But it didn't "just happen": *it had been happening for some time.* There were *trends* involved. Though we do not always see the whole picture, life flows inexorably through all that happens, *as* all that happens.

The explanation is in what we are calling *trends*. *Trend* could be another word for *consciousness*. A trend is a tendency in a certain direction, a predisposition. Planet Earth, which is our home, is always in a state of flux. Global ecologists are worried about a warming trend in the earth's atmosphere and a shrinking trend in the rain forests. Politicians view with alarm the latest information about voter trends and demographic movements. Economists talk about market trends and the fluctuation of the stock market.

The only thing static about our life is our thought about it. We are always in the flow of life. We are always moving toward our good, or away from what we have perceived to be our good. Our health reflects a wellness trend, and sometimes, sadly, an illness trend. The wise student of life works to take charge of his/her life by controlling thoughts and emotions. It is not a matter of "bucking the trends" but rather understanding and rightly directing them. A trend is not "just the way things are." It is an indicator of *your attitude* about the way things are. It is a *positive trend* (**positrend**), if you are focusing on that which is good. It is a *negative trend* (**negatrend**) if your mind is hung up on the negative.

"Living in the fast-lane" is a modern-day cliché. The pace of our lives is characterized as "fast," "quick," "instant," "express." We are promised "instant" relief by a particular brand of medication, "instant" youth from a face-lift, "swift" check-out in the express line; gardeners call grass sod "instant happiness." So many people live with a dizzying schedule, running from one activity to another, almost as if they feared missing something.

We refer to "the tempo of city life." We seldom realize that our lives are dominated by this tempo. We need to slow down and listen to the rhythm of our own inner drummer, and march to its beat. Today we can travel long distances in short periods and do tasks in a fraction of the time it once required because of new technologies. But the questions we need to ask from time to time are "What do we do when we arrive at that distant place we traveled to at such a frantic pace? What do we do with the time we save with our labor-saving devices?"

In Central America a railroad was being built by American engineers. A native carrying his crops to market on his back stopped to watch the construction. He asked an engineer what they were doing. The engineer explained that the railroad would enable the farmer to get his produce to market and return in one day, instead of the three days each way now required. The native said, "But señor, what will I do with the other four days?"

We often find ourselves like the White Rabbit in Lewis Carroll's *Alice in Wonderland*, running about crying, "I'm late, I'm late, I'm late." But the problem is, we aren't really late. We are in a hurrying trend and are out of tune with the larger meaning of life. We need to slow down and let the soul catch up with our bodies.

Whenever you are late, or think you are burdened with urgency, something has gotten out of tune. Rushing will not reestablish that attunement any more than racing your engine will get your car back into gear when it has slipped out. The need is to pause, take a break, and take a time of quiet reflection on the allness of God in which you live, and . . . watch the feelings of rush and hurry—and the related fear—slip right out of mind.

The Prodigal Son out in the far country was living in the fast lane, spending his inheritance in his quest for meaning, trying to find himself even while increasingly losing his self-respect, driven by "affluenza" and enslaved by conformity to the world "out there." He ultimately came to know want. But the important thing finally happened: he "came to himself." He realized who he was. And one thing is for certain: he was in the wrong lane.

Continuing with the metaphor of lanes on a highway, we may crawl along in a slow-moving lane, irritated and frustrated. But then we may "come to ourselves," saying, "I don't have to take this. I can change lanes." And so, changing lanes, we are suddenly in a new milieu. Of course in real life, changing lanes will not change a condition until we have changed the consciousness that is causing it. Wherever you go, your consciousness goes with you. You do not jump from misfortune to good fortune, or from illness to wholeness. Changing lanes is an *opportunity* to change the experience. If you want to get there, you must earn the right to be there.

Realizing you are in a lane that is a stream of negative thinking and feeling, you have the freedom and privilege to "change lanes." This is knowing and participating in the ever-present and active stream of creative ideas. *This* is the natural highway for the spiritual being; it is the path of your journey. *Change lanes.* Move easily into that stream of energy. You are not creating it, but, as co-creator, you are choosing to cooperate with divine law. You will be outpicturing in your world the creative intention that is uniquely expressing as you.

Take a day for personal research. Make a con-

certed effort to watch your thoughts. Look for a
repetition of experiences. For instance, you might
find yourself thinking, "I will never be able to make
it." You have established a trend. And things will
conspire to make your words prophetic. Or you might
find yourself with thoughts of optimism and faith: "I
have a lot of faith that I am going to succeed." This
is a *positrend* that will tend to attract to you the
means of achieving a successful conclusion.

We usually take *negatrends* too lightly. For instance, you may reveal a trend toward hurt. This
would mean that you are hurtable. It will be as
though you had an antenna that picked up every
slight, every criticism, every act of thoughtlessness.
And you *would* be hurt—often. Search yourself. You
may be unaware that you have a trend toward hurt.
You can change this attitude by formulating a *positrend*, an affirmation of strength and nonresistance,
such as, "I am centered in love and I project a radiance of love. I refuse to let other persons decide for
me how I am going to act and react" or "I am poised
and centered in Infinite Mind, and nothing and no-
one can disturb the calm peace of my soul."

To understand the trends of our lives, we need to
understand how mind works. Thought for most persons is a reflex process. Things happen and we react
to them in thought. We become worried or fearful or
happy or inspired or sorry. We assume that thought
is produced by circumstances. But experiences do not
cause thoughts. An incident happens, there is no
denying it. It is history. But as far as you are con-

cerned, the incident is completely external . . . the reaction is your own. You think what you want to think, or what you have habitually thought. So the first step in learning how to think is knowing that no matter what happens in your world, you always have a choice. You do not have to be angry or disturbed. You can choose to think positively and creatively.

With many persons there is a kind of laziness in thinking. The human race has proved to be a race of lazy thinkers. It is much easier to let someone else do our thinking for us—and most persons do just this. The true progress of the human race has almost invariably come through a few great thinkers who have occasionally appeared on the scene. And the majority of people have followed long behind—resulting in *trends* of human behavior.

Now the problem with lazy thinking is what I call *drifting*. In the book of Hebrews we read, "Therefore we ought to give more earnest heed to the things that were heard, lest . . . we drift away from them." When the mind is not alert, creative, positive, working toward a definite end, we find ourselves drifting in the tide of human events, of generally accepted concepts, or what Charles Fillmore calls *race beliefs*.

In this sense, most of us deal in second-hand thinking. The great thinkers, philosophers, and teachers may set forth a wave of powerful creative ideas, which in turn become the trend in popular conversation. For a while we may float along on their influence. Then we tend to drift away. As Shakespeare says through his Julius Caesar: "There is a tide in the affairs of man, which taken at the flood leads on to fortune, omitted, all the voyage of their life is bound in shallows and miseries."

How much of our life is bound in shallows and miseries simply because we have drifted along on the tide of negativity? How many people drift along with the tide through life, hoping for better things, but never doing much about getting them, thinking that "things are as they are, and there isn't much you can do about it"?

Imagine, if you will, sitting in a small rowboat in the mouth of a river, drifting with the incoming and outgoing tides. The current of negative thinking is sometimes overwhelming. In order to accomplish anything in life, one must take up the oars and row ceaselessly against the tide—the tide of public opinion, the tide of achievement barriers. How easy it is to accept as inevitable the drift of age and deterioration, the drift of physical conditions that come along with certain stages of life. How easy it is to drift along with beliefs concerning world conditions: economic upheavals, recessions, depressions, "downsizing" lay-offs.

There are two things you can do to prevent a boat from drifting: (1) you can anchor the boat and (2) you can pull sturdily on the oars. Often we drift because we do not row; and we do not row because we have never determined where we are going. We are aimless.

I once had a profound lesson in a simple experience. I was scheduled for a lecture in an unfamiliar town. The train was late, so I jumped into a taxi and said to the cabbie, "Please drive as fast as you can; I am terribly late." So the driver raced off at breakneck speed. After a few minutes I said to the driver, "Aren't we about there?" He replied, "I don't know, sir; you never told me where you want to go."

How many persons lead hurried and harried lives, racing here and there, frantically changing lanes, like trying to find the shortest line at the bank, but never stopping to ask themselves where they are and where they really want to go and then plugging in to the spiritual power and guidance to lead them forward.

Many persons say they want to change, but the closest they come to real change is moving into another lane. However, the lane has no magical power. Remember the move to the new lane is only the *opportunity* to change. But as I say often, "The Universe can do no more *for* you than it can do *through* you."

The mind is in constant motion, like the ocean, ceaselessly moving, ebbing and flowing, drifting. When we talk of controlling the mind we do not mean control in an absolute sense, but in a regulatory sense. We can't turn it off. (Sometimes we may wish that we could!)

Many centuries ago, Oriental thinkers compared the mind to a "jumping monkey" and said that the first step in getting control of the jumping monkey is to *let* it jump. Just stand back and watch it objectively: you will observe that it is not you. You are not the mind, but you may stand behind it and use it as an instrument. And when this realization is firmly in consciousness, you will be on the verge of self-mastery.

Positrends or Negatrends? is a book for all seasons. It is not just for entertaining reading (though we hope you will be entertained too). We see it as giving you a perspective from which to deal creatively with the Millennium and to enter into the "Golden Age" of life on the planet with joy and enthusiasm.

➤ Common is the practice of compartmentalizing one's religion in a particular section of the brain, with the practical and intellectual in a different compartment, and "never the twain shall meet." We have used the religious segment only in church or in prayer. We now know that we have sacrificed the *greatest* source of creative power; and in our worship we have practiced the *absence* of God. Our God "out there" is willful and vindictive, and we are in the position of having to beg and plead for divine help.

The Ground of Being

In our count-down to the Millennium, we want to consider the trend to deal with God anthropomorphically as a person, and mentally as an intellectual construct. There is no way that we can become a fully functioning person, and an integrally creative unit in a dynamic Universe unless we find and know God. In this respect we will consider an idea that is both simple and profound. It is simple in that it is uncomplicated and practical. It is profound in that it contains the secret of the ages, the key to understanding ourselves and fulfilling ourselves.

In her novel *Pilgrim's Inn*, Elizabeth Goudge says through one of her characters, "His religion had never consisted in more than believing in God, without ever having asked himself what he meant by God." When you use the word *God*, whether in believing or in doubting, what do you mean?

Most of us have grown up under the influence of a picture of God as the great Ruler of the Universe, sitting on His throne "up there." You may think of *God and you*—but close as He may be to you, it is still God *and* you. Healing is something you get God to do for you. But if God can do things for you, He can also be too busy doing things elsewhere. If He can heal you, He can also bring, or acquiesce in, illness. If He is one with whom you can negotiate, He might say No!

The trend has been to think of religion as institutions instead of perceptions . . . something you join rather than a transcendence you experience. We need occasionally to refresh ourselves with the vision of Paul's sermon on Mars Hill (Acts 17): "The God who made the world and everything in it, being Lord of heaven and earth, does not live in shrines made by man, nor is he served by human hands, as though he needed anything, since he gives to all men life and breath and everything. . . . Yet he is not far from each one of us, for in him we live and move and have our being."

How could the "God-of-the-skies" perception have survived such a clear revelation?

The perception of God is complicated by the distinction between considering God objectively and considering Him subjectively. If you think of God *objectively*, He becomes to you a person living "up there" or "out there," a person possessing human characteristics. He is a God who may will to help or to hinder, to give life or take it away. However, if we think of God *subjectively*, we do not see God; *we see from the consciousness of God*. This is implied in Jesus' Beatitudes: "Blessed are the pure in heart, for they shall see God." (Note: if you see through rose-colored glasses, you see all in a rose tint.)

It is difficult to think of God as a person who is omnipresent, but if you think of God *subjectively*, you are like a searchlight, projecting a beam of light to all that might concern you. It is the key to the new insight into prayer.

Religious studies seem compelled to render a definition of God. But whoever gives a definition of God announces to all who have ears to hear that he or she doesn't understand the spiritual process. He may know a lot *about* God, but by putting his knowledge into a closed definition, he indicates that he doesn't really *know* God.

The *idea* of God is really a great *idea*. We build an intellectual construct about Him (or Her or It). It is a three-letter word, G O D. Santayana calls it a "floating literary symbol." We worship it, we express love and devotion to it. And we build imposing theological structures on it. But still it is all "out there." The key is, do you know *yourself*?

Let's turn to the words of Aldous Huxley in his *The Perennial Philosophy*:

> It is because we do not know who we are, because we are unaware that the Kingdom of Heaven is within us, that we behave in the silly, often insane, sometimes criminal ways that are so characteristically human. We are saved, we are liberated and enlightened by perceiving the unperceived good that is al-

ready within us, by returning to our eternal
ground and remaining where, without knowing it, we have always been.

Huxley is suggesting the need to be grounded, or
else, as Emerson puts it, we may "Soar to the em-
pyrean heights, and dive to the unfathomable depths,
but never pay cash." So "the Ground of Being" indicates that in which we are rooted and in which we
live and move and have our being.

The first of the Ten Commandments has usually
been understood as implying a personal God "out
there," setting down the rules for living: "I am the
Lord your God, who brought you out of the land of
Egypt, out of the house of bondage. You shall have
no other gods before me."

If we view these words as tradition has interpreted
them, the mind runs inescapably toward billowy
clouds, a regal throne, a majestic figure with a long
white beard, and a booming voice crying out, "I am
The One, and you had better believe it!"

In seeking to expand our God-concept, we need to
confront all the legends and symbols and myths of
our religious faith that keep us from the experience
of communion. One such symbol is the "Ark," which
was supposed to house God. The Israelites carried
God with them in the Ark as they went forth into battle. If it should be captured, they were shattered. In
time the Ark was safely ensconced in the Holy of Ho-
lies in the temple of Jerusalem—which soon became
known as "the house of the Lord."

Today that idea still persists. Great throngs of people stream into churches and synagogues across the land to get close to God. But if you should feel the Presence of God in that sanctuary, it is because *you* are there; and you are there (or should be so) not to worship God at the altar, but to celebrate the Truth and experience a sense of "creative worthship." You are a spiritual being, and the Kingdom of God is within you. You are a worthy channel for the expression of wisdom and creativity and love and perfect healing life. Emerson, a great religious curmudgeon in his day, startled people with his suggestion that we break with the God of tradition and cease from the God of our intellect, that God may fire us with His Presence.

One way of getting a workable understanding of God is to think of Principle, from which you cannot possibly be separated. Consider gravity—can you be dislodged from the gravitational field on earth? In the new physics we know that the subatomic particle is not just a bit of cosmic dust that has been swept up and held in place by the force. It *is* the force acting *as* a particle, and it has no existence outside of the force. In the same way, you are not just the creation of God, molded and shaped and set out on the path of life "down here." You *are* the Presence or the Allness of God expressing Himself or Itself *as* you, and you have no existence outside the Presence or Allness of God. You may be separated in your thoughts of fear or anxiety, but there is no way you can ever be less than an identity or individuality within the Allness of God. The power of the Whole is always present.

There is a principle that I call *Unitivity*. The great fact about unity is that because it is a single unity, wherever it is at all, the whole of it must be. If we talk about one part of the unity there and another part here, we lose the idea of unity. Because it is infinite and limitless, it is everywhere—and the whole of Spirit must be present at every point in space at the same moment. Wherever you choose to concentrate your thought, Spirit is present in Its entirety. There is no spot where God is not.

What a difference it would make in the life of a child if we could get this concept through to him or her early in life, so that it might be carried as a consciousness all through life! I have a dream that a day will come when institutions of higher learning will recognize Unitivity—the unity principle—and will build their educational programs on the complete integration of knowledge with the *knower*, of creation with the creator. The student should never lose sight of the thread of spiritual unity—whether one be in the laboratory, the observatory, or in the chapel.

Recall Huxley's "Returning to our eternal ground and remaining where without knowing it we have always been." This ground of being is a philosophical way of referring to the sea of infinite possibilities, in which we live and move and have our being. This ground is a fertile field of mind, where we exist as seed ideas, and as long as we keep ourselves grounded in the awareness that we are in the ceaseless flow of life, intelligence, and creativity, we shall experience abundant life.

I refer often to that great insight of St. Augustine,

"God is a circle whose center is everywhere and whose circumference is nowhere." In a moment of imagery, pick a spot to focus on. It may be a relationship or some problem or emergency. Get the image of being in space at the center of a circle that is the Universe, and out from you there stream in all directions rays of light projecting to the farthest reaches of the Universe, which has no end. The center is everywhere (where you are) and the circumference is nowhere. There are no limits of time or space—or of life, love, or wisdom. The center of the dynamic Universe is there in the midst of the problem. And, as Plotinus says, "The whole Universe comes rushing, streaming, pouring into you from all sides while you sit quiet."

Until you realize and begin to practice this Oneness —which means God *in* you expressing *as* you—your God is not great enough; and this deficient God-concept will give rise to all sorts of doubts: How could God allow the baby to die, or the earthquake to ravage the area, or the accidents to occur? And you will mistakenly look at God through your challenges, almost insisting that your God must prove Himself.

But God is not a performer who must continually prove Himself worthy of the role. God is changeless Principle, the ultimate "bottom line." These two words are the most overworked in our time. You may be discussing assets and liabilities, and the possibilities of succeeding in some project, and it will be said, "But the bottom line is . . ." Figures may be given to justify the negative appraisal that there is just no way you can accomplish it. The "bottom line" suggests an "irrefutable fact"—the last word. It is impossible, and that is that.

Jesus said, "Judge not according to appearances, but judge righteous judgment." Just imagine that you have an acorn in the palm of your hands. You have been told that there is an oak tree in this acorn. Skeptically, you take the acorn apart and analyze the meat, do all sorts of chemical tests on it, concluding that the analysis of the oak tree is false. The bottom line of intellectual perception is: an acorn is an acorn —not an oak tree. However, beyond the bottom line there is the reality of nature's growth process in that seed. It is demonstrable: you can plant the acorn in the ground and witness the growth into a sturdy oak.

As the acorn germinates in the ground and grows into the oak tree that it is designed to become, so the divine idea that you are is planted in the Ground of Being, the field of limitless possibilities. And as you focus on your innate divinity, you experience a progressive releasement of your divine potential.

The great idea that Jesus articulated and demonstrated is the idea of *God in you*. He said that the Kingdom of God is within you. However, we must be careful lest we lose the thread here: God is not in you as a raisin is in a bun, or as a pearl is in an oyster shell—for the raisin and the bun remain separate entities, and the pearl and the oyster are always two different things.

God is in you as the ocean is in a wave. The wave has form and shape and movement, but it can never be less than *ocean*. And there is no way you can remove a wave from the ocean. *This is oneness*. Similarly, there is no way that you can be separated from God. The wave is the ocean expressing as a wave, and you are the activity of God expressing as you.

If you expand this ocean-in-a-wave metaphor from the persepctive of a fish, where is the ocean? One thing a fish can never find is the ocean. It could be said that the ocean is nowhere, which you will note is "now here." And God is nowhere if you are trying to find or contact the "Green Pastures" kind of God —a majestic figure in white robes, lolling on white, billowy clouds. But if you "be still and know," you will find that God is *now here*, not meeting you from without, but flowing forth from within; not just doing things *for* you, but working *through* you and *as* you.

This explains a Bible paradox that has confused people for ages. John 1:18 says, "No man hath seen God at any time." Yet in the Beatitudes, Jesus says, "Blessed are the pure in heart, for they shall see God." "No man hath seen God" relates to the "God is nowhere"; "the pure in heart shall see God" relates to the "God is now here." God is not a person to be found anywhere; yet when you get an awareness of The One and your oneness in it, you begin to see with a spiritual perspective, you see from God-consciousness—and you see God in all persons, and in all experiences.

In Sanskrit the word *eye* is *ayin*, which literally means "fountain." This is the key to the most creative kind of seeing: a spiritual perception. The eye does not simply record impressions received from "out there." The eye is a fountain that projects con-

sciousness like a searchlight. In the highest kind of
seeing, you simply look at someone and he or she
feels a healing influence. You don't have to raise
prayers of exhortation for the one about whom you
are concerned. You need only get centered in the divine flow, look at the person (even if separated by distance), and behold the perfect child of God.

Of course this challenges you to get a new insight
into prayer. Prayer is knowing the Truth, realizing
oneness. It is dealing with the God-is-now-here metaphor. The old idea was that prayer was a means of
trying to reach God somewhere "out there" in the
nowhereness of space to try to get Him to solve our
problems. But the Truth idea is that we want to understand the principle of Oneness—and our oneness
in the One—so that the Presence is present *as* us.
Then we draw upon the infinite potential within us
by which we solve (or dissolve) our own problems.

I once received a letter from a member of my ra-
dio audience. He was a minister who often criticized
my talks. The interesting thing, however, is that he
was listening. He accused me of "destroying God,
reducing prayer to bold, brazen affirmations." But
how can anyone destroy God or even reduce Principle in any way? What I do is challenge people to destroy their limited intellectual construct of God, so
they can know God as a principle and as a presence.

I suggested to this minister that he look up the
meaning of the word *principle*, for the dictionary
says: "A source or cause from which a thing proceeds, a power that acts continuously, or informally

—a permanent or fundamental cause that naturally or necessarily produces certain results on all occasions." In other words, *changeless reality.*

You may say, "But how can you pray to a principle?" You don't! Which may challenge you to a new insight in prayer. Prayer is knowing the Truth, meaning oneness. The old idea was that prayer is a means of trying to reach God and get Him to solve our problems. The Truth idea is that we want to understand the principle so that we can solve our own problems, or dissolve them.

Note how Jesus prayed; did he stand at the tomb and plead with God to return his friend Lazarus? No! He declared his oneness with God . . . and then he cried out, "Lazarus, come forth!" How could he be so sure? Well, why is the mathematician so confident of the mathematical principle? Simply because it *is* principle. He knows it is unerring.

We would never think of blaming the principle of mathematics for an error in our computation. And it simply never occurred to Jesus to trace the death of Lazarus to God. He said, "It is not the will of my Father that one of these . . . should perish."

Jesus used the sun as a symbol for God. It causes its rays to fall on the just and the unjust alike. It glints into the hospital cot, the prison cell, the palace and the hovel—anywhere the person admits it. So with the God-principle: there is quite simply no spot where God is not. And we cannot exhaust Principle. Every man, woman, and child in all the world could be using Principle at the same time without exhausting it one iota. So with healing and overcoming. And in Principle, every person is God expressing as them.

This was Jesus' great discovery: the divinity of man. Everyone is an eachness within the Allness which is God. Our mission in life is to unfold more All-ness, to release our imprisoned splendor. It is not try-ing to get into God, or to get God into us; rather it is to "Be still and know that I am God."

In the New Millennium there is an increasing need for persons who consciously choose to "practice the Presence of God." Every person is a child of God, a child of the Universe. Only a few know it, and fewer succeed in expressing any marked degree of the per-fection of the indwelling Christ. Instead, when our God-self is concealed and frustrated, we experience the shadows of human consciousness—and then mis-interpret them as outside evil forces. We need to say, as Jesus said, "Get thee hence . . . for there is only one God, and Him only will I serve."

I love the vision and imagery of Wordsworth as he describes his sense of the God-presence:

A sense sublime
Of something far more deeply interfused,
Whose dwelling is the light of setting suns,
And the round ocean and the living air,
And the blue sky, and in the mind of man;
A motion and a spirit, that impels
All thinking things, all objects of all thought,
And rolls through all things.

PosiTrend:

*I am established in the consciousness
of God present and active in every part
of my mind, body, and affairs.*

*God works in me and through me
and I work with Him
in the wisdom and power
of Spirit.*

*There is a universal creative intention
for me and for all that I desire
to see manifest in my world.*

*Whenever I feel blocked
I quietly listen to the divine intent
and the door to my good opens
and I am on my way.*

➤ Work in our day is experiencing a "marketplace revolution." Companies are being dramatically "downsized." Jobs are being eliminated. Prediction: Less than half the workforce will be in full-time jobs at the beginning of the 21st century. We say, "It's just a weakness in the economy. Business will come back, along with a return of our jobs." But most businesses are doing fine, and the jobs are gone forever. "Change is avalanching on our heads, and most people are grotesquely unprepared to cope with it."

CHAPTER

2

*In*trepreneurship*
for Everyone

When an important project is undertaken, a company organized, or a structure erected, the common thought is that it is always personally beneficial to be "in at the beginning." When we think of this day as the beginning of the structure of the rest of our lives, it is good to be "in at the beginning." This is not just referring to being present, for we can't do much about that. We are alive, we are here, and that is that.

*See p. 19.

But there is another, more important, factor. Life is lived from within→out. And if we are centering our attention "out there," in the future, looking forward in resigned expectancy to "more of the same"—*or* squinting forward, seeking a prophetic glimpse of a predestined future—then we are out of touch with reality.

To be "in at the beginning" is to be centered in the consciousness that the coming year (or decade or century or millennium) exists as a series of opportunities to grow, to unfold the infinite possibilities that are enclosed within every person.

We want to deal creatively and realistically with the Millennium. *Positrends or Negatrends?* is an inventory of some of the problem areas of our society (negatrends) that we see to be the result of negative streams of consciousness. But there is something to do about them (positrends). It all comes down to attitudes—*our own.* Let's consider our attitudes about work.

We might as well face it: we *are* going through a marketplace revolution. The days when a job was the sole means of financial security are over. Jobs are being permanently eliminated. We shall have to begin taking charge of our own security. Rewards and promotions will be going to the one who does the best quality and quantity of work—not the one with the most seniority. Workers will need to think of themselves as entrepreneurs, as contract workers. They will need to get the idea of service, of looking for work beyond the parameters of their job.

We are seeing an increasing emphasis in the marketplace on creativity and productivity. We are being informed that the "job" will not be a part of the emerging economic reality. Although there will always be an enormous amount of work to be done, that work will not be contained in the familiar activities we call jobs. In an out-and-out economic revolution, many organizations are today making great strides toward being "de-jobbed."

The job is an artificial social phenomenon. From primitive times up through the ages, we see no evidence of the job. The job concept emerged early in the 19th century to package the work that needed to be done in the growing factories.

Now the place of work is being re-evaluated. Mass production gave rise to the technology that gave us automation, and robotics led to a production line minus all those job-holders who used to do their repetitive work.

A prominent economist recently said that less than half the work-force in the industrial world will be in "proper" full-time jobs in organizations at the beginning of the 21st century. It is a startling prediction, but it simply reflects the trend in the marketplace.

Studies into the causes of economic instability often refer to the "work ethic." This involves the jobs you get and the compensation and retirement benefits you get through them. I have coined the term "*worth* ethic," which deals with your primary quest for a sense of self-worth, which in turn is enhanced by your job and not compromised by it.

To the ancient Greeks, work was a curse. It was also the curse on Adam and Eve for disobeying God: they were condemned to work by the sweat of their brow. The Greek word for work was *ponos* ("sorrow"). So for many persons work is downtime—something to make the best of, to endure. To better understand ourselves and the work attitudes we have been conditioned to, we might turn back and consider the Industrial Revolution, in the 18th and early 19th centuries. With the development of the steam engine, the discovery of new sources of power, and the invention of many new machines, the agrarian society that had prevailed for ten thousand years on earth was transformed into modern industrial society.

The Industrial Revolution turned humankind away from nature, resulting in the mass urban setting, for which society was not adequately prepared, which in turn led to the breakdown of the ecological system so much in evidence today: slums, smog, and air and water pollution. The Industrial Revolution shifted human values to the measurement of life in material and pecuniary terms.

Our interest is in jobs, where we can earn a steady income along with health and retirement benefits. What we may not be aware of is that the job is a social artifact created by the Industrial Revolution to package the work that needed to be done in the emerging factories. But as the industrial machines have given way to "hi-tech," the bulk of the work is being done by computers and robotic systems. Giant corporations are downsizing their workforces. And we fail to see what is going on if we say "It's just a time of weakness in the economy. Business will come back, along with a return of the jobs." Many of these businesses are doing fine—and the jobs are gone forever.

During our lifetime we have been conditioned to lives built around jobs. We have talked of "good jobs" and have positioned ourselves to climb the corporate ladder rung by rung—job by job. We have been blind to the fact that jobs discourage accountability. We have been rewarded not for *getting the work done* but for simply *doing our job*. This may entail clear parameters: often heard is the cry, "That isn't my job!" Yet the *realistic* employee asks not, "Whose job is it?" but "How can I help get the work done?"

A word we are hearing more and more today is *entrepreneur*: by definition, a person willing to go into business for him- or herself, venturing capital, time, and talents in taking charge of their own economic life. I use the term *intrepreneur* in reference to those persons who are imaginatively seeking to redesign their attitudes toward work, effectively altering their work without changing their jobs.

Work is often something we have to do to earn the money to enable us to enjoy the "good life." The "good job" has come to mean the high salary, and career success is judged by the bottom line of net worth. So education or "job training" is something we do to prepare us to get the "job"—not necessarily to grow in it. And sadly, it could be said that the peak of a person's education, training, skills—even motivation—is reached shortly after being ensconced in the job. In the smug feeling that he has completed his education, he settles into the work which he soon admits he could do with his eyes closed; and even if he persists in the belief that he can be an innovator, more often than not he encounters a choking mine-field of company policy and precedent. The old hand takes him aside and advises, "You have to understand how we do things around here."

It is likely that Adam once said to Eve in the Garden of Eden, "My dear, we are living in a period of rapid and accelerating change." Most of us have an inbred fear of change. There is great and growing fear of the changes implicit in the coming Millennium. In the Industrial Era, which we can almost refer to in the past tense, one would learn a trade or a profession and expect to practice it in roughly the same way for the rest of one's life. This is no longer the case.

We may have been influenced by ads that proclaimed, "Earn a trade and secure your future." The choice was between different ways to go; and once the choice was made, there was a road all laid out for us, building houses or operating a drill press. There was a hesitancy to take the road less traveled, for there would be no assurance of health benefits and retirement funds and life-long job security. We might get bored with the routine of the job—however, life would be predictable.

But times have changed. Example: in the "smoke-stack industries," thousands of men and women who have worked all their employment life in one job, developing and perfecting a single skill, are suddenly laid off, facing the prospect that the job will never return. They may be too young and financially insecure to retire, yet facing a societal attitude that they are too old to get another job. They may feel faced with a choice between going back to school to learn new skills and going on welfare. But now, with the new changes in welfare "as we have known it," the options are slim.

The answer: become an *in*trepreneur. Make a commitment to take charge of your own life. You can't always control what happens *to* you, but you can control what happens *in* you—your reactions, your moods, your expectations. You can maintain a calm assurance of security even in the face of a job layoff.

As an *in*trepreneur, you carefully avoid the trap of looking to your employer for your security. You know that your security is always with*in* yourself. In other words, you must build an unshakable conviction and consciousness that your true business is the "express business"—the business of expressing or outforming the creative flow within you. You know that you are working for God, with gratitude to the company as a channel through which opportunity for work and compensation flows.

The worker of the future is likely to require a great deal of flexibility, not just one set of skills acquired early and good for life; rather it will be an evolving body of knowledge and new opportunities calling for greatly modified skills. Lifelong learning is no longer a desirable luxury; it is a vital economic necessity. The *intre*preneur carefully builds into his consciousness the realization "I do not resist change, but I adapt myself to the law of *'All things work together for my good.'*"

I believe that a job change is a helpful and healthful challenge. It might be good for everyone to make a change every ten years . . . otherwise we become lethargic, complacent and self-satisfied. We need the challenge of change to keep us youthful and vital and productive. One way to determine whether you have been in one place too long is to ask yourself: "Have I had ten years of experience—or one year's experience ten times over?"

There is the classic story of a man consulting with a career counselor. He was not fulfilled in his work. Asked if there was anything he had always dreamed of doing . . . he had always regretted he didn't go to medical school and become a doctor. "Then why don't you go back to school? You are single with no responsibilities." "But with medical school and hospital internship, it would take me seven years. Then I would be too old." "And how old will you be in seven years if you do not go back to school?"

The whole economic system in the world is changing. Many of us have idealistically looked forward to a futuristic arrangement where we would work less and less and have increasing time for recreation. Unfortunately, we haven't realistically envisioned the personal responsibility involved. What's happening is, companies are becoming smaller, with fewer and fewer "soft" jobs squirreled away in the halls of the corporate structure. The businesses of the future are streamlined for efficiency, with a minimum emphasis on "job description." A thing of the past will be the observation "TIMJ" (that isn't my job). Today's organization is rapidly being transformed from a structure built out of jobs to a field of work needing to be done.

It is kind of scary to contemplate having to shoulder the responsibility for our work life. We have looked on the entrepreneurs as daring adventurers investing their capital, time, and talents in taking charge of their economic life—and ours! But the business world that is evolving is calling for entrepreneurship for everyone. We must get used to the idea of being in business for ourselves and of being more like external vendors than traditional employees.

That is why we have been using the word *intrepreneur*, referring to the person who is imaginatively seeking to redesign his attitudes toward work. This is not in the future—it is *now*.

We need to get a new attitude toward work. Friedrich Froebel (1782–1852), a German educator and founder of the kindergarten system, had a refreshingly positive sense of the cosmic process at work in the individual. How good it would be if his idea of work could be stressed in our educational system!

> The delusive idea that people merely toil and work for the sake of preserving their bodies, and procuring for themselves bread, houses,

and clothes, is degrading and not to be encouraged. The true origin of a person's activity and creativeness lies in one's increasing impulse to embody outside of oneself the divine and spiritual element within.

You occasionally hear someone describing a job that has been taken to "get by," saying, "Oh, it's a living." But in this consciousness it is anything but a living. It might be more accurate to characterize it as a "drab existence." In this consciousness the worker is actually cutting him- or herself out of the creative flow.

Any job can be the means to a lifetime of frustration if we think of it simply as a way to earn a living. More accurately, it should be a way to *"learn a living"*—a place to make a life, to grow, to unfold as a person. Life is a growth process, and we grow through giving. No matter what the circumstances, if you ever do less than your very best in what you may be doing—no matter what the recognition or reward you may receive—you are storing up what the East calls "bad karma."

When things do not work out for you, you may wonder, "What is wrong with me? Why do I not get ahead?" It is an example of "pigeons coming home to roost." It is a matter of consciousness. There is no way that prosperity may manifest outside the law of consciousness. You may say, "But I do all that I am paid to do." But do you do all that you *can* do? If not, you have placed yourself in opposition to the laws of the Universe.

The average person sets out to make a success in life, working hard, keeping on . . . experiencing hardship and setbacks . . . but picking up and going on nevertheless. The successful person is not one who has never had a defeat but one who has never been defeated. A handicap or reversal is a good excuse to give up, if you have a failure consciousness. But it is a good spur to achievement if you have forged a mentality that vibrates with the good, the prosperous, and the successful.

We are in the midst of a worldwide economic revolution. We are surrounded by paradoxes. An alarming number of people are out of work, yet businesses are doing quite well. People are waiting to get their jobs back, but in fact the companies are downsizing and the jobs have been eliminated. The unemployment rate can be at an alarming high, yet the stock market can also be at an all-time high. The modern world is on the verge of a huge leap in creativity and productivity—but the "job" is not going to be a part of tomorrow's economic reality.

Become an *in*trepreneur. This refers to attitudes, spiritual ideals, and a consciousness of the *"worth ethic."* It means carefully avoiding the trap of looking to your employer for your security. The day when the "company" provides the security, hospitalization, retirement, and the host of employee benefits may be nearing an end. *Your security is always within yourself.* It is knowing that your true business is the "express business," the business of expressing or outforming the creative flow within you. It is knowing that you are working for God, with gratitude to your employer as a channel through which opportunity for work and for compensation may flow.

Twenty years ago Alvin Toffler in his book *Future Shock* wrote, "Change is avalanching upon our heads, and most people are grotesquely unprepared to cope with it." Only the *in*trepreneur will be equipped to face the unknowns of the Millennium with confidence and security.

The New Millennium beckons you to walk forward through the gate of the year into the golden era of your life. The Universe is calling, and it is a calling to your life-work. God works in you as your creative potential, and you work with Him in the wisdom and power of Spirit. "The best is yet to be."

PosiTrend:

I resolve to take charge of my work-life.
I can't always control what happens to me but
I can control what happens in me
—my reactions, my moods, my expectations.

I can maintain a calm assurance of security
even in the face of a job termination.
I know my security is always within me.

I establish myself in the consciousness
that my true business is the "express business"
—the business of outforming the creative flow
within me.

I am working for God
in gratitude to my employer as a channel
through which opportunity for work
and compensation flow.

I meet the changing conditions of the economy
in the realization that
"I do not resist change, but I adapt myself
to the law of 'All things work together
for my good.'"

➤ We have tended to make a god of the doctor; and health-care is something that is done *for* us. We need to take charge of our life and assume total responsibilty for our health-care. The question is now being asked: "Is the symptom the byproduct of the illness; or is it a causative influence that gives rise to the illness?"

There is a proliferation of talk of "bugs" that are "going around." One medical specialist refers to "psychic infection" and the "contagion of fear."

Managing Your
Own Health-Care

There is much talk of restructuring the nation's health-care system. We have the finest care available in all the world, but our delivery system is woefully inadequate, and at a cost that puts it out of reach for the average person.

But the greater need is reshaping our attitudes toward personal health-care. Many of us have grown up with a family doctor to whom we looked for care in all our physical need; but that is an era now past. In the millennium to come, we shall have to take charge of our physical life. We shall need to acquire knowledge of nutrition, proper exercise, stress-management, and the most effective means of therapy. And we shall need to understand and practice the metaphysics of holism.

With all the controversy surrounding the health-care systems in America and the need to make radical changes, the tendency is to overlook the fantastic changes that are occurring in attitudes toward healing on the part of the medical profession and the religious establishment. We are in the midst of a healing revolution, born of the discovery that we are spiritual, mental, and physical creatures—a discovery as profound as the Theory of Relativity.

In the long years of civilized history, the efforts to reestablish health for a person experiencing illness have been locked into primitive beliefs and superstitions. Our theologies may have become more sophisticated, but the ignorance of the way life works has been profound. Illnesses are laid on us by fate or God's will or from "natural causes." And healing has involved a long list of therapies with dubious results, or through prayer to mollify God's will, or to experience a healing miracle.

In the 20th century there has evolved the discovery of the dimensions of mind (subconscious, conscious, and superconscious), the impact of thought upon the body, and, more recently, "the mind-body connection." This has given rise to such terms as "alternative methods of healing," "psychosomatic healing," "behavioral medicine," "Psychoneuroimmunology," and "holistic medicine."

Many theologians are experiencing the breakthrough from the rigidity of the religion *about* Jesus into the dynamic power of the religion *of* Jesus. It is being increasingly believed and taught that Jesus 2000 years ago revealed the principles of spiritual healing. "The Kingdom of Heaven is within you"; you are a spiritual being with a healing process built into your body temple.

An important prerequisite to understanding the healing revolution is the realization that healing is not something that is done *for* you or *to* you. Rather it is something that happens *in* you and flows *through* you. And the foundation on which it rests is the "wellness process." I use the term *wholing*. It is a process grounded in the awareness that health—real health—is from within and does not have to be manufactured in the without. In other words, it is not a matter of *defeating illness*, but of *releasing wellness*. Wholing is dealing with life in the attitude that wellness is as natural and simple as a smile . . . as normal as a flower or a sunrise.

The diagnostician focuses essentially on symptoms. To him they point to the illness. Then the doctor proceeds to treat the symptoms. Today a question is frequently being asked, one that would once have been ludicrous: "Is the symptom the byproduct of the illness—or is it a causative influence that gives rise to the illness?"

Illness is not something we *have*, but something we are *doing*. And the symptom may give us the best insight into what it is that we are doing. What is being repressed? It may be conditions that you do not think you can cope with.

The symptoms may be telling you what you need to eliminate in your thinking and feeling. They may be telling you where and how you have repressed the energy that is life, blocking its free flow into expression. Drugs and medication may soothe the symptoms, but we are coming to realize more and more that only you, as you get in touch with yourself and give way to the cosmic healing flow, can eliminate the symptoms and experience the fulness of life that it is your nature to have.

Dr. Wallace Ellerbrook says very bluntly, "If you get sick, it is because you have been thinking screwy." He says that diseases in the body are behaviors—not things that happen to you, but things that you do.

We talk of "catching a cold." (Like "catching a pop fly to the infield"). The important thing is, *don't* catch it! Don't get into conversations about the "flu season" or the "bug that is going around." One doctor talks about "psychic infection" as one of the major causes of illness.

It could be said that you do not *have* arthritis—you are *arthritising*. You do not *have* an ulcer, you are *ulcering*. You do not *have* cancer, you are *cancering*. You are participating in it. This isn't all bad, for if you participate in the condition, you can participate in the healing.

We say, "I am nursing a cold." You are *colding*. On the other hand, *wholing* is what you do in terms of a positive strategy for directing your mind and emotions in creative support of the cosmic healing flow, e.g., loving and forgiving, engaging in things that make for wholeness, including rest and good nutrition.

Dr. Hans Selye said that one thing all patients have in common, whether they suffer from cancer or measles or indigestion, is that they all *look* sick. Their faces show that they don't feel well. He wondered for 30 years why we shouldn't study the syndrome of "just being sick," reasoning that if we could cure that syndrome, which we might call *sicking*, it wouldn't matter what caused it, for the sufferers would soon be *wholing*. It was this insight that gave rise to his revolutionary concept relating to stress as the prime root of illness. Dr. Selye was an important forerunner in the field of psychosomatics and the more current study of psychoneuroimmunology.

Stress is often cited as the major cause of illness today. But stress is not something that comes from a job or a relationship or the problem of coping in today's world. It is your reaction to these things, your resistance, your envy, your worry. You are *stressing*.

When we witness the renewal of life in the garden at springtime, or the steady growth of a child, or the healing of a cut on the finger, we feel a compelling reverence for the mystery of renewal. This is what life is all about. The cells of your body are constantly being renewed, which means, for example, that you actually have a new finger every three to five days. The cells of your eyes are renewed every eight to ten months. It could be said that your body is never more than two years old.

One of the things we have working for us is what Paul calls "the Lord's body." I call it *the counterpart body*. We are told, "God created man upright [whole] but he [man] has created endless subtleties of his own."

God's creation is a perfect body—perfect in a spiritual sense, despite any imperfections of the human form. In a very real sense, there is a divine will or creative intention to outform that perfect heart or liver or stomach.

A medical doctor treating a physical ailment does not alter this process. He works with what he calls the *vis medicatrix naturae* ("the healing power of nature"). The wise practitioner does not think of himself as a healer. He knows, as a French doctor once said, "I bind the wound; God heals the cut." If it were not for this basic healing power, the slightest nick with a razor would cause a person to bleed to death. As it is, the cut is closed by the action of hemoglobin in the blood. Were it not for the wonderful provision of white corpuscles and antibodies in the bloodstream, and the opsonins that render harmful bacteria powerless, we would succumb to the first attack of germs. The entire art of medicine is based on the knowledge and predictability of this natural healing force.

Dr. Richard Cabot, dean of the Harvard Medical School many years ago, speaking before the Massachusetts Medical Society, said, "I remember an autopsy on a man killed in an automobile accident. He had never been sick a day in his life and always felt in perfect health." However, he found that the body was harboring four usually fatal diseases; yet the body had set up defenses that rendered them all harmless.

"The body simply has a super-wisdom that is biased on the side of life rather than death. It is ten times more powerful than medicine. What is this powerful force? It is God. And I urge the medical profession to let the patient know of this great force that is working within him or her. It does the doctor no good to avoid the word *God*. Why not teach people the Truth?''

And the Truth is there is a Cosmic Healing Flow that is present in its entirety at every point in space. It is a healing activity that Yale University biologist Edmund Sinnott refers to as "the natural configuration of the whole." An acupuncturist calls it *vital energy*. The evangelist may call it the *Holy Spirit*; while the yogi calls it *"prana."* Call it what you will, it is the Cosmic Healing Flow. It is the power that heals. It is God.

After many years of the practice of prayer on the healing activity in the human body, I have come to the conclusion that the fundamental difference between spiritual and medical healing—the different techniques aside— is one of time.

Medical healing deals with the constant process of cell renewal, conforming to set time schedules (i.e. skin cells renewed in 3 to 5 days, etc.). Spiritual healing, on the other hand, deals with consciousness, which transcends the limitations of time and achieves a rapid acceleration of the renewal process, so that the result may appear to be instantaneous, as in the case of a "miraculous demonstration."

But before we explore this distinction we want to acknowledge the role of the mind in health and physical well-being. The Bible says that God has made people upright, but they have created endless subtleties of their own.

Think for a moment of sunlight streaming through a window. The window may be small, opaque with dirt, or tinted with stained glass. In each case the light shining into the room is shaped and shaded by the aperture through which it comes. Outside, the light is present in its fulness. Inside, it becomes to us that which the window allows. Life is whole. Life cannot be sick or old . . . and life can never die. Life is the energy through which Spirit manifests itself as us, but always to the degree of our conscious acceptance.

Paul obviously had this in mind when he said, "Not discerning the Lord's body, many among you are weak and sickly." "The Lord's body" does not refer to Jesus' body, but to the embodiment of the law of life, "Christ in you, the hope of glory."

In other words, what we call illness is a distortion of "Allness." Even as light is a present reality though the window shades be drawn, the Allness of you, the Christ of you, is still present even if concealed. It can be said, then, that you are whole even when you are weak, sick, or in pain.

Now let's return to the time factor in healing. We live in a three-dimensional world, caught up in a belief of time and space. When the doctor gives his prognosis that a healing will take three months, he is not dealing with absolutes. He is basing his forecast on case histories of similar ailments. Jesus said, "You say it is three months until the harvest, but I say unto you, lift up your eyes, for the fields are now white unto harvest." He was indicating that the Christ consciousness transcends time.

When you touch the inner springs of being in deep inner prayer, you not only release forces of renewal into the body to reverse physical ills, but the healing process is stepped up and "nothing shall be impossible unto you." When Jesus healed the man lame since birth, there was a breakthrough in the mental image of affliction, followed by a great acceleration of the cell renewal process. It was like speeding up the recording of a symphony so that a full hour's rendition is heard in one grand chord.

There is a constant process of renewal of the cells that works according to a meticulous time schedule ("three months till the harvest"). But there is also a nonmaterial level of life where the desired healing is already a reality. "Before they call I will answer."

We always invoke the healing process according to our consciousness and according to whether we are working with medication or meditation. The healing may take three weeks, one day—or it may be instantaneous. But in every case the "mystery of renewal" is the healing force and its process.

All healing is natural. There is no healing miracle in the sense that the healing power of nature is bypassed or voided. The human body is always biased on the side of life. God doesn't deal in miracles. God is the wholeness of life, substance, and intelligence that is always present.

It is not a miracle that is needed, but the discipline of consciousness to let "Thy kingdom come, thy will be done, on earth as it is in heaven." Paul said, "Be ye transformed by the renewal of your mind." He did not say, Be transformed by having a miraculous power possess you from the outside. No! "By the renewal of your mind."

This leads to the practice of affirmation in healing treatment. The body may be sick and in pain, but you can and should declare, "I am whole." You can affirm this truth without hypocrisy, even while a medical specialist is working on you. For you live in two worlds, not serially but concurrently. Your physical body is subject to physical processes. The medical practitioner works on this part of you. But at the same time, in the Allness of you there is a non-material body that is perfect and whole, which is the key to the healing process.

It is my belief that the only distinction between medical healing by the continuity of cell renewal over a fixed period of time and the paranormal demonstration of healing by prayer or metaphysical treatment is in the transcendence of time. The only time is now! Life is now! Any unfoldment that *can* take place *is*!

Thus you can affirm the already present existence of anything that you seek to demonstrate even if the healing effort is being made with medical assistance, and especially if it is. Realize that while the doctor works *on* you, the transcendent force of life works *in* you. *Know that there is an Allness even within your illness.* Do not be dissuaded by a prognosis of time. Claim your oneness now!

Get the feeling that the cells of your body are like a household of children in need of discipline and direction. Talk to your body. Bless its functions. Praise it for good performance.

PosiTrend:

My body is the temple of the living God.
I accept full responsibility for its care.
I balance the knowledge
of the metaphysics of holism
with the knowledge and practice of nutrition,
proper exercise, stress-management
and the most effective means of therapy.

Real health is not a matter
of defeating illness
but of releasing wellness.

The body has a super-wisdom
that is biased on the side of life
rather than death.

If a doctor is working on you
know that the transcendent force of life
is working in you.
There is always an Allness
even within any seeming illness.

negatrend

➤ Rampant prejudice . . . intolerance of minority groups . . . the grim specter of "ethnic cleansing." Emphasis on differences between people— "and never the twain shall meet." Lack of understanding of the meaning of love. In prayers for peace: "We would have inward peace, but we will *not* look within."

The Relationship Revolution

As we prepare the way for the entrance into the Third Millennium, into what I am calling "The Golden Age" of life on this planet, we are considering some of the *negatrends* of human consciousness that call for corrective action.

The world, once considered so vast, has shrunk in size to a "Global Village." And in a global sense, we will have to get along with or destroy one another. Prejudice and intolerance are still very rampant in America, and there are wars of "ethnic cleansing" being waged in the world, revealing the ugly extremes to which the "race problem" can take us.

There really are no race problems—only *people* problems. Jesus said, "Love thy neighbor as thyself." Honestly, now, do you "love your neighbor as yourself?" If you do not, you have a problem. Solve your problem, and to that degree the race problem is solved.

One of the best-known stories of the Bible is the Genesis account of Noah and the Flood. It is chiefly allegorical. However, mention of the Flood occurs in the literature of many cultures, so it is likely that something of the kind did happen. At any rate, one of the great enterprises of all time was the building of the Ark to preserve the best of life on earth. Humans were an endangered species!

Noah did his job well and they all rode out the storm, but in the end Noah missed the boat. His purpose was to eliminate a profligate human race and start over—but to no avail; for as soon as the waters subsided, Noah planted a vineyard and made some wine and got drunk. So the human race was right back where it had been.

In the story, the descendants of Noah journeyed East, where they found a plain and settled. But modern Bible scholarship agrees that this is a mistranslation. It should be, "The people journeyed *from* the East." This makes a tremendous difference, for the Bible message is veiled in symbolism. "East" refers to the inner, the spiritual, the divine. "West" refers to the outer, the material, the sensual, the worldly.

So when the sons of Noah journeyed *from* the East,

they were falling away from their spiritual roots, setting materialistic goals. This was evidenced as they began to build a tower—the famous "Tower of Babel"—which they wanted to reach all the way up to God.

They were feeling the "upward pull" of the divine potential within. They wanted a relationship with God. But they were thinking of God "up there" and "out there." They were trying to have a relationship, but in a totally superficial way. And it says, "But the Lord scattered them abroad from upon the face of all the earth, and they ceased from building the city."

A great goal for the people of planet Earth in the New Millennium is to resolve the confusion that sets us apart and find the way to communication between people of diverse backgrounds. The word *Babel* literally means "confusion."

A classic cliché that has been accepted through the ages as a universal law is that you can't get people of different cultures or groupings to agree. The Bible asks, "Can the leopard change his spots?" Kipling has been quoted as an authority on the subject by reason of his "Ballad of East and West." ("Oh, East is East and West is West, and never the twain shall meet.") It is a cliché that has been used in support of prejudices of all kinds. But it is a classic example of a twisted meaning derived from taking something out of context.

For in Kipling's "Ballad of East and West," he actually says:

Oh, East is East and West is West
  And never the twain shall meet
Till earth and skies stand presently
  At God's great judgment seat.
But there is neither East nor West,
  Border nor breed nor birth,
When two strong men stand face to face
  Though they come from the ends of the earth.

So Kipling is actually saying, "The twain *shall* meet." In a very real sense, there is no East or West, no Oriental or Occidental, no black or white or yellow or red, no rich or poor, male or female—when we stand face to face with minds open to the flow. One mankind, one world, one divine creation.

In our preparation for the Third Millennium, there is a great need to return to the "East," to get recentered in the Presence within, to remember that we are spiritual beings growing through a human experience. Now we are not calling for a "return to religion." That is a cliché that often justifies building more towers of Babel. Religions are all too often gaudy lamps with no flame, humanistic theologies that skirt or deny the Spirit.

The need is not for the return to ecclesiastical religion, or for the creation of new religions. The need is for people, one by one, to make the journey from the West to the East—to return to the awareness of the Spirit in every person. It is not a question of church or religion or creed. The lamps may be many and varied in shape and design. But when the oil is kindled in the lamps, the many flames give off the same illumination. We need lamps that are lit, not just owned and looked at. This was Jesus' call: "Let your light shine." While we strive to find ways to solve the conflicts between nations and individuals, we must be sure that we bring a light instead of simply cursing the darkness.

Occasionally religious organizations or groups of individuals sponsor a World Day of Prayer for Peace. It may be a commendable effort. However, in most cases the prayer is judgmentally based. We have talked about "those people over there" who are causing the problems. We say, "People are all alike! What can you expect from them?"

So we have a great day of "praying" for them—hoping they will change their ways. Prayer efforts such as these are not very productive, for they are usually rooted in prejudice. A prayer for peace is ineffective unless it commits the pray-er to become a channel for the expression of the infinite love of God.

Getting along with people is not so much dependent on them as it is on your *going along* with the flow of love. It could be said that getting along with another person is only 2 percent about what he is and does, and 98 percent about how you react to what he is and says and does.

"What the world needs now is love," we romantically sing. But the question is, what do you do when people are *not* loving? How can you love someone you don't even like? But love is not an intensive of the verb *to like*. You may think that your love is in scant supply when it comes to those people. You may say, "I have tried very hard to love, but I just can't." Of course you can't! For to *try* to love is *not* to love. Love is not *trying*—it is *being*.

We must work for an understanding that love is not the plaything of human volition, but the action of divine law. Love does not begin in you and end in the object of your love. It begins in spiritual law, flows through you, and there is no end.

Love is not a commodity that is passed from one person to another. You don't love just because you are loved, and *only* if you are loved. You love because "He first loved you." Because God is love within you and you are created as an outlet for its flow, love always flows forth from within you to the degree that you let it. And there is no limit.

There is always enough love to go around. In any relationship it is your nature to love, unless something in your consciousness blocks the flow. Love comes as naturally from you as radiation from uranium. Prejudice is normally the culprit. I believe that prejudice is the strongest single cause of upsets and upheavals in man's inhumanity to man.

The original meaning of *prejudice* was "preconceived opinion without knowledge." It is being positive about something negative without good reason—a lazy person's substitute for thinking. A Sunday School teacher asked her class for a definition of prejudice. A little girl said, "It means deciding some guy is a stinker before you even meet him." Since no one is born with prejudice against anything or anyone, it follows that these feelings are unwittingly passed on by parents and other adults. In his *South Pacific*, Oscar Hammerstein wrote of prejudice, "somebody taught a child."

In some respects the passing down of meaning from one generation to another is time-saving. But we inherit not only the wisdom of the ages, but also the misconceptions and distortions. A university professor, no less, was heard to remark that he never got over the feeling of surprise when someone he admired turned out to be a Republican. The emotional conditioning remained despite historical thinking to the contrary.

To love at first sight or hate at first sight, and then interpret succeeding events as a proof of our intitial judgment, is backward thinking. Love at first sight is dangerous because we have associated something with the person and therefore expect too much of them. Here is a statement that I have used to keep a balanced perspective among all casual or intimate contacts with people: "If I knew you and you knew me, we would love one another, regardless of who I am or who you are."

You simply cannot hate a person you really know, but you can't really get to know a person whom you view only through a haze of prejudice. Hitler was a German, but so was Goethe. Mussolini was Italian, but so was Michelangelo. The great, significant differences between us are not racial; they are individual.

Each one is a person, and we must so treat them.

I like to restate the Golden Rule in this way: "I will treat others as I like to be treated; I will treat them as individuals, as people, as children of God. I will take time to get to know them, to respect their ways, their limitations, even as I expect others to have patience with my own weaknesses."

When we consider the need to make relationships of love everywhere, Cain's eternal question comes to mind: "Am I my brother's keeper?" In recent years we have answered in the affirmative, as can be seen in our many social welfare programs. The flaw here is that we have administered benefits, yet retained prejudice toward anyone who takes advantage of them. The overriding problem of contemporary social action is that one group is trying to work *for* the other group instead of working *with* the other group. We give money and service, we write checks and do volunteer work—but do we give brotherhood?

You may say, "Of course I have no prejudice. I have been active in the promotion of 'Brotherhood Week.' " During Brotherhood Week we are supposed to be nice to people, to treat all people kindly, in effect to say to people of minority groups, "You know we love you, don't you?" But what happens when the week comes to a close? More than likely it is back to business as usual.

Why not have a "Hate Your Neighbor Week"? Get it all out of your system in seven days of prejudice and ill-will. Then spend the other fifty-one weeks treating all people as human beings. Just kidding— but not entirely. It is something to think about.

"Am I my brother's keeper?" I say, "Absolutely not!" I have no right to be anyone's keeper, and to attempt this only leads to a loss of dignity and pride—and therefore to much resentment. Rather, *"I am my brother's brother."* Emerson takes it an additional step: *"I am my brother, and my brother is me."*

One of the mysterious facts of life is that every individual in this world stands alone. Each person is a unique grouping of atoms called "I." This atomic grouping is the basic minority group. Just as no two atoms ever really touch one another, so no two individuals ever completely touch each other, no matter how closely they may be thrown together. Even in the most nearly perfect union of man and woman, there are always some reserves, some barriers, something withheld.

Under all the differences that we allow to separate us, there is a unity that binds all persons into one great whole. The essential fact in human history is the slow awakening all over the world of a sense of unity, the gradual unfolding of a feeling of community between all persons and between all nations, and between all races, nationalities and ethnic groups.

Humankind has been dispersed to the far corners of the planet, but through modern means of communication, the human creatures are coming back into one great whole. This will increase dramatically in the New Millennium in a veritable *relationship revolution*.

The unity of all humankind is scientifically true. The human race with all its differentiations goes back ultimately to one common source. From that source, through prehistoric times, early peoples wandered to and fro, extending their migrations ever farther across the earth. And the differences that exist today between the various races of humans—differences in color, in physical characteristics, in manners and customs, in language, in religion, in dress, in government—all developed gradually through long periods of time and due primarily to differences in environment, climate, food, soil, etc. But difficult as it may be for some persons to accept, the biological basis of humanity is one; the same blood flows in all our veins. It has been said before, and it should be said today and at all times to come: *It is one world!*

The urge for freedom and equality is as natural and fundamental as gravity, or water seeking its own level. During the years when there was little communication, people could live or be made to live under certain conditions in relative contentment. But modern electronic communication has changed all that. Everyone now has a chance to be a part of the "good life."

The world is on the march for unity. It is a march that can never be long repelled, only understood. Communism was a part of this basic march, but it was a principle misapplied. Christianity was essentially a unity movement, but it lost its way in the development of churchianity.

People have imagined—wrongly—that they are private selves, living separate lives, and having separate fates and destinies. This is the grand illusion that has given rise to all the disunity in the world since civilization was born. The great challenge, then, is for everyone to look beneath the externals and recognize the Super Self in all those whose paths cross ours, rather than beholding and reacting to the surface selves with which we are constantly coming into conflict.

Someone might say, "But if I held this attitude toward all people, it would leave them free to take advantage of me, since they are still living in surface consciousness." As a matter of fact, if we would only dare to treat people not as they appear to us, but as they really are in their deeper selfhood, it would do more to help them to discover their true self than all the preaching or lobbying or social action in the world.

In the next hundred years, when the dust has settled from the relationship revolution, the world will be a kinder and gentler place. The age of violence will be dissolved in the healing energy of transcendental love. Resolve to be a part of a new age (Now age) of gentleness.

PosiTrend:

I am in the flow of transcendental love.
I AM the flow.
I give way to its healing energy
wherever I am in consciousness
or in relationships.

I let go of the last vestiges
of prejudice and intolerance
and relate to all persons
in the spirit of brotherhood.

Let there be a great wave
of love and brotherhood
reaching out like ripples
in a pond to people everywhere
and let it begin with me.

➤ When pressure exceeds our limits, the resulting stress leads to a breakdown of the immune system and to susceptibility to a host of physical ills.

If you lose your inner center and become immersed in the things of the world, you will be pushed and pulled, and you will feel lost, for you will have no roots.

Often the cause of pressure and strain is the burden of responsibilities, the clock and the calendar, the economy or world conditions, the fear of the future, worry over the past.

Dealing with Stress

As we enter the golden era of the New Millennium, we need to be conscious of the Cosmic Healing Flow. It is an exciting concept, dealing with the idea that every person is created and sustained by a dynamic process, a transcendental flow of life. No matter what condition may manifest in the body temple, it is biased on the side of life.

Basic to this insight is the awareness that no physical limitation just happens. In some way we participate in the illness, and in the same sense we can participate in the healing.

One of the common ways by which we frustrate the healing flow is through the much-discussed influence of *stress*. We hear the term so often that it would appear to be some new disease. However, it is likely that the early caveman, trying to exist in a world dominated by giant creatures and unpredictable elements, experienced great stress.

Today, over 100 years after the metaphysical movement began teaching about a strong mind-body link, there is a growing acceptance in the medical community that the emotions are necessary components of the cause, as well as the treatment, of most illness. Difficult to let go has been the general orientation of the medical profession that physical ailments are produced by physical causes and should therefore be treated by physical intervention.

The research into E.I.I. (Emotionally Induced Illness) and stress has indicated undeniable mind-body relations. But it has understandably had to accept them in a medical context, with a new, fancy 21-letter word, *psychoneuroimmunology*. So today, whether the physician or the metaphysician is talking, the advice may be the same: "Let go of stress."

Most of us are all too familiar with what is called the "pressure syndrome"—the high tension levels built into our life and work. The stress may come in many ways: a multimillion-dollar financial crunch for the executive, two term papers on the same day for the student, a make-or-break audition for the performer seeking a role, or simply dealing on a day-to-day basis with the high cost of living.

But when pressure exceeds our limits, creativity disappears, errors multiply, and life becomes difficult. But what is most important, the stress leads to a breakdown of the immune system, and to susceptibility to a host of organic ills.

An Eastern scholar made this comment on the life of people of the West:

> It is impossible for the mental life of a person to unfold normally towards a state of enlightenment, unless the physical environment be simplified in every possible way. Confusion, stress, interruption, noise, and the constant vibratory agitation present in the surroundings of the average occidental, make it practically impossible for him to have a balanced and normal existence.

Today it has been found that the link between stress and illness is so strong that it is possible to predict illness based on the amounts of stress in people's lives. This work was originated by Dr. Hans Selye of the University of Montreal. It has been proven that when a patient suffers a major emotional upset, there is an increase not only in diseases usually felt to be susceptible to emotional influence (ulcers, high blood pressure, heart trouble), but also in infectious diseases, backaches, even accidents.

A study was made to develop the means of objectively measuring the amount of stress or emotional upset in a person's life. Numerical values were assigned to stressful events. For instance, the death of a spouse was given the value of 100; personal injury or illness, 63; change in financial status, 38; trouble with in-laws, 29. The researchers found that 49 percent of those with a total of over 300 in a year contracted some form of illness. Almost as interesting was the discovery that in 51 percent of cases the 300 + score did not result in illness. Which seems to underscore the value of positive coping strategies for dealing with stress.

Stress has become such a popular subject that, along with the common advice to relax and let go, there are many sure-fire coping techniques offered— from hypnotic suggestions to chucking it all to go and paint in far-off Tahiti, with numerous misadventures with Valium or Prozac along the way. We apparently try almost anything to ward off the recurring crunch. Yet the answer is as close as the creative use of our imagination. For stress isn't produced by things that occur. It is the thinking and feeling about them that give you that gnawing, head-in-a-vise feeling.

The stress response to conditions is a learned response. You can *un*learn this response by eliciting a physical relaxation response. In the same way that you have learned to speed up your biochemical processes when you are aroused, you can learn to slow the processes down and return your body to a normal balanced state.

Researchers may offer exercises, sometimes called "coping strategies." When you find yourself becoming irritable, tense, and easily overwhelmed, what you need is not just a coffee break. You need a break for prayer, or a silence, or a meditation.

Medical researchers have long recognized that *silence* plays an important role in healing. Doctors will often prescribe bed-rest and quiet for most ills. It is doubtful if the medical person realizes that the real benefit lies in getting recentered in the universal flow. One analyst says that human life needs at times to steep itself in silence, from which it may draw its essential nourishment and in which it develops its deepest roots. It is a matter of getting centered within yourself, which is the finest strategy for coping.

It is important to know that we always have a choice in every happening, whether we are going to curse the darkness or bring the light; whether we engage in fretting or letting; whether we will experience tension, stress, or strain in the face of things, or keep centered in the poise and strength of the Christ Mind within.

An excellent affirmation to hold is: *"I am poised and centered in the Christ Mind, and nothing can disturb the calm peace of my soul."*

In this way you can walk easily through any experience "out there" without conflict or pressure. But if you lose your inner center and become immersed in things of the world, you will be pushed and pulled until you feel lost, for you will have no roots.

A great self-treatment that I use as a means of coping with symptoms of stress is this:

> *I work without strain and walk without hurry, for I am in tune with the rhythm of the Universe. That which needs to be accomplished will be done at the right and perfect time and in the right and perfect way.*

One man made this discovery for himself. He says, "I am bigger than anything that can happen to me.

All these things—sorrow, misfortune, suffering, and all the burdens of responsibility—are outside my door. I am in the house, and I have the key." In other words, *"I am in charge."*

Jesus says, "In the world you have tribulation. But I have overcome the world." *Tribulation* comes from the Latin word meaning "press." In other words, "In the world you have pressures, but I have found the way to cope."

This was one of the great things Jesus taught: the only problems you ever have are in your own mind. "A man's enemies are of his own household." No matter what happens out there in the world, or even on your doorstep, all that counts is what happens within your own mind. Get your thoughts positive and your mind at peace—and nothing can disturb you.

When you are centered within yourself, you walk easily through things, for *you* are in charge—not the clock or the calendar, not the economy or world conditions, not the fear of the future or worry over the past. In the world there may be pressures, but you can cope.

It is like a baseball pitcher who is aware that there are five innings left and his team is five runs behind. He could easily be pressured by the feeling that he must pitch "no-hit ball" in the remaining innings. And even then his team must come up with some runs. But if he is a pro, he will simply concentrate on the one inning at hand, and the one pitch he is going to throw next.

There is the subtle weakness in having clearly set

goals and well-outlined "master plans." Unless one is careful, these things can produce great pressure and strain. Of course have a plan, and keep it in the back of your mind. But don't worry about it or let it become an obsession. *This moment* is all you have to work with. The past is behind you, the future is yet to come. A goal is not a preoccupation for tomorrow but a direction for today. If you want to protect yourself from the strain of anxiety or the fear of failure, be certain to keep yourself *"now-minded."*

Often the cause of pressure and strain is the burden of responsibilities—often associated with our work. One man told me of something that threatened to curtail his career. He was brilliant, hard-working and had had a meteoric rise to a high executive position in an important corporation. He had to make frequent snap decisions involving many millions of dollars. One bad decision could cost the company a fortune. He nearly broke under the strain, spending many sleepless nights second-guessing decisions he had made during the day.

I helped him realize that guidance is a spiritual law. Emerson says it is the continuation of the process that made the person in the first place. Thus he didn't have to *make* decisions—only to *discover* them. This took all the pressure off him. It proved that *conditions* do not make the pressure; it is the way we meet them that creates the pressure.

Some interesting research was done at DuPont Nemours. They were seeking to determine whether executives are at high risk of heart attack because of pressure. It was discovered that executives and plant managers had an annual heart attack rate of only 2.2 per 1,000—while the manual-worker's rate was 3.2, and the clerical worker's 4.0. It just could be that people become executives precisely because of their ability to withstand stress.

In other words the tensions of responsibility do not necessarily shorten a person's life. As the researcher's report summed it up. "Stress cannot be measured by the external circumstances with which a person must contend . . . but rather by his reaction to these circumstances. One person's stress may be another person's pleasure." Tension, stress, and strain come not from things that happen, but from our way of dealing with them.

I once stood before the beautiful statue of Jesus by the Danish sculptor Thorvaldsen, which he calls "Come unto Me." The story is told that he wanted to create the greatest figure ever made of Jesus. He fashioned a commanding figure of great strength, with a fine, well-shaped head thrown back imperiously, and with arms raised in a gesture of domination and command. He left the clay model in the studio with the windows open wide.

During the night the fog and sea-mist "did a job" on the unfinished work, transforming its character. When Thorvaldsen returned the next morning, he found that the head had fallen slightly, so that the figure was looking down with an expression of compassion. The arms were no longer raised in a gesture of command, but were lowered in an attitude of welcome. The figure still showed great power; but instead of dominion, it now expressed love and service. Thorvaldsen at first was disappointed, thinking that his figure had been ruined. Then, after a period of reflection, he realized that this was what he had meant to portray. And he named the sculpture "Come unto Me!"

This is what being centered in the Christ consciousness does for us. It softens the features made hard by material thinking and relaxes the muscles made taut by the stress of worry and anxiety.

The physical pose of modern people engaged in making a living and carving out a place in the world may well be symbolized by the first conception the artist had of Jesus: commanding, demanding, aggressive, and willful. Life for these people is all push and pull and struggle and strain. They have an attitude that often displays a brash confidence, and they may even achieve a kind of success—but it is built on the sands of materiality. Jesus pointed out that a house built on sand would fall under the pressure of crises.

However, when Truth comes into the consciousness, you find an almost spontaneous relaxing of your human hold on life and things and people. You get off the "scurry-go-round" in the marketplace and begin to work in the realization that there is no competition —that there is abundance for all. You work with diligence and sincerity, but without strain. And the challenges of life are met not at the *expense* of your resources, but at the *expanse* of them.

We need to take time (make time) for relaxation and change of pace. An American woman was visiting an exhibition of Chinese art. She was taken by one picture, depicting a tree with very few branches and very few leaves, with much space between the branches and a bird sitting on one of them. The woman said to the Chinese artist, "I would like to buy that picture, but would you paint in a few more branches and leaves?" The artist replied testily, "Oh no, for that wouldn't leave any room for the bird to fly."

Do you have room in your life to live? Do you have room in your busy schedule for change of pace? For relaxation? For inner silence? The need of every person, especially one who must deal with the demands of life in the marketplace, is to take time every day, and at least two times every day, to "Steep yourself in silence, from which you may draw essential nourishment and in which you may develop your deepest roots."

This practice will help to keep you consciously centered within yourself, so that you can keep up a busy schedule, carry heavy loads, and produce great amounts of work without strain or pressure. For there is a place of central calm at the eye of every storm. Thus there is always a center of repose within any arena of work.

In this consciousness you can depend on an inner guidance to make decisions easily. You can trust the process to evolve creative ideas. You will work without strain and walk without hurry, for you will be in tune with the rhythm of the Universe. And you will be open to the unimpeded outforming of the Cosmic Healing Flow.

PosiTrend:

I am poised and centered
in the Christ Mind
and nothing can disturb
the calm peace of my soul.

I work without strain
and walk without hurry
for I am in tune
with the rhythm of the Universe.

That which needs to be accomplished
will be done at the right and perfect time
and in the right and perfect way.

Stress cannot be measured
by the external circumstances
with which a person must contend
but rather by his or her reaction
to those circumstances.

One person's stress
may be another person's pleasure.

negatrend

➤ The destructive power of negative speech.

The most pious people have indulged themselves—at times other than in worship —in words that express negativism, pessimism, and fear, and then wonder why bad things happen to them.

The inability of many persons to put two words together without a word of profanity.

The Toxic Effect
of Words

The subtitle could well be "Verbal Toxemia." The word *toxic* means "poison." Through medical research, we are becoming aware of an increasing number of substances that are toxic to the physical system. And to that list we are adding *the toxic effect of negative words*.

A little boy was pushing his baby brother in a stroller. A kind woman admired the baby, and said to the boy, "What a handsome child! Can he talk?" The boy replied, "No; his words haven't come in yet. But he has two teeth."

When his words do "come in," he will be faced with a responsibility for taking control of one of the most important functions of human consciousness.

Through all the ages people have sought magic words by which they could summon riches, fame, power, love, or any other great thing they might desire. Thousands of ancient legends, fairy tales, and stories have told of wise men, witches, and fairy queens who have had command of secret phrases that could accomplish miracles.

So it is that thousands of years before the development of modern psychological knowledge, human beings of virtually every race and place recognized the power of the spoken word to change their circumstances and their lives. Of course we now know that there is no power in "abracadabra" or "open sesame." But there is tremendous cosmic power that flows through us, which may be frustrated or expressed through the character of the words we use in our daily living.

Jesus was keenly aware of this power when he warned us that we could be defiled by the words we spoke and that we would be judged by every idle word we uttered. He said, "not that which entereth into the mouth defileth the person; but that which proceedeth out of the mouth. . . . And I say unto you that every idle word that people shall speak, they shall give account thereof in the day of judgment; for by thy words thou shalt be justified, and by thy words thou shalt be condemned." (Pretty strong stuff!)

There is a fairy story about two sisters, one "good" and the other "bad." When the good sister spoke, pearls and diamonds and precious things dropped from her tongue. But when the bad sister spoke, snakes and bugs and creeping things fell from her tongue. A wise mother explained the fairy tale to her daughter in this way: She said that the precious stones were loving, positive, beautiful words—and that the snakes, bugs, and toads were unkind, sorrowful, and negative words.

If, like Job, you have been plagued by physical or financial problems, you may be asking, "Why?" And, like Job, you may feel that you are a victim of some "cosmic frame-up."

Remember, Job tried to reason with God, trying to convince Him that he was a good man. But he overlooked one thing: that the laws of life are exact, and that "goodness" covers more than conformity to religious practices. After going through some horrendous experiences, he eventually made a great discovery: that his sin was not so much his manner of living as his manner of speaking. Job was a good man, but he was probably guilty of slovenly speech. He may have lived an exemplary religious life, but if his everyday speech was centered in worry, fear, and resistance, he was exhibiting "verbal toxemia."

It is amazing how we take speech for granted. We learn to speak, for the most part, without conscious effort. And by the time we are mature enough to understand those strangely powerful and dire noises we call speech, it has become so much like reflex behavior—like breathing or coughing—that it hardly occurs to us that there is anything about it to understand. Thus, most of us never do understand our speech in any comprehensive way. *We just talk.*

The church that you had your religious conditioning in was strangely silent on the energy of speech. It just never came up. So even the most pious people have indulged themselves, at times other than in worship, in words expressing negativism, pessimism, and fear.

This is additionally strange since the power of words is extolled throughout the Bible in some of the most beautiful language ever written: "Whoso keepeth his mouth and his tongue, keepeth his soul from troubles." "Set a watch, O Jehovah, before my mouth; keep the door of my lips." And then, perhaps the most beautifully descriptive statement in the entire Bible, "A word fitly spoken is like apples of gold in a network of silver."

It is interesting how many Christian tenets are not found in Jesus' teachings at all, and how many things powerfully stressed by Jesus are conveniently overlooked. For instance, his powerful statement, "I say unto you that every idle word that people may speak, they shall give account thereof in the day of judgment." He is not referring to divine caprice, saying that God won't tolerate negative things, that they grate on His nerves, and that He will punish offenders with a divine slap on the wrist. Idle words are words spoken only for the pleasure of the passing moment, from the nervous habit of talking to avoid silence. They are spoken from personal consciousness with no thought of their reaction on the speaker or their effect on the one spoken to.

Jesus is outlining spiritual principle. The "day of

judgment" is not some future millennium when the "roll is called up yonder." It is now! It is the moment when we realize the effect of the laws we have set in motion by our negative words. And the toxicity of negative words is poisonous to the system.

In the teaching of practical metaphysics, we normally focus primarily on the power of thought and the function of the subconscious mind—completely overlooking this important matter of speech.

Dealing with truths of mystic power, many persons still allow a steady stream of negations to fall unchecked from their lips. It is a perfect example of negatrends that spew forth poisons that are toxic to the body and that foreshadow a trend toward failure in our affairs.

One woman was talking about how she was having problems with her eyes. She said, "I am just not seeing very well." But then she added, "I can't see why I should have trouble. I spend fifteen minutes every morning, affirming that I have perfect sight. She has created a jingle that she sings in her periodic prayer-times:

> I'm free from tension, stress, and strain,
> My eyes are wide and bright.
> I know the Truth that sets me free,
> And I have perfect sight.

It is an excellent treatment, if you can establish the idea in consciousness, and if you can cause the affirmations to come together with feeling, and if you "pray without ceasing." But if you sing the jingle once a day, and then only perfunctorily, you may deserve what this woman's husband called her Pollyannaish parroting: "Esoteric hokum!" Words of Truth have no power of themselves. They are empowered by your faith and feeling. Your words become vessels for the outpouring of spiritual energy as you become synchronized with the Creative Flow.

The phrase "I can't see" has become toxic in the life of the woman with vision problems. She often says, "I can't see why people act in that way," "I can't see why I don't get that salary increase," etc. "I can't see . . . I can't see." I would say to this woman, "You can scarcely expect to demonstrate perfect vision in those fifteen minutes of constructive affirmation, when the rest of the time you are affirming that you can't see. You will protest that you don't mean that you actually can't see. It is just an expression that you have a habit of using."

Infinite Mind is as impersonal as the soil. If you go into your garden with a package of pansy seeds with which some weed seeds have gotten inadvertently mixed, does the soil raise its faithful little hands in horror, exclaiming, "She doesn't mean to plant those weeds, so we won't do anything about growing them"? No. The weeds are grown and brought forth in all their glory as tenderly as are the pansies.

It is strange how many students of Truth think they can declare affirmations of positive power in moments of spiritual seeking—and then think that what they say at other times doesn't count under divine law. The practice of Truth is not just a matter of building up a repertoire of powerful affirmations of Truth for use in emergency situations. Perhaps it is this for some persons, but there is so much more. You are a whole person, and consciousness pertains to all your thoughts and words —not just those expressed in selected times.

The man ridiculed his wife's practice of Truth as "esoteric hokum." She was forever spouting affirmations, seeming to feel that what she said at other times didn't count. It was like saying, "time out." But there can be no "time out." The subconscious mind doesn't discriminate. It can't tell the difference between your *causal* and your *casual* thoughts. You may insist that when you said, "That burns me up!" you were only kidding. However the subconscious mind can't take a joke.

Words that are negative have a toxic effect on your life. You may begin having fevers that you can't account for. They are simply "the judgment day" for your idle words—like *"That burns me up!"* This is because spiritual law operates through our consciousness; and when consciousness projects itself in words, spiritual law becomes a specific law that we have set in motion—a law that works relentlessly to convey the energy that we have vested in it, no matter that the words were negative. It is as if we created little toy sailboats and invested them with the power and direction of sailing, and then turned them loose. They would continue relentlessly until we pulled them out of the water.

Every statement we make about ourselves or about conditions in general is a subtle kind of prayer. For instance, you may have habitually said, "I always catch a cold in the winter." And it is correct: you always do. Not that you are a prophet or that you are honestly addressing a personal weakness. Your statement actually sets up a law of being, which governs the manifestation of life for you.

There are many laws at work in our experience, which amount to a personalization of cosmic law. The course of our lives may be strewn with countless little perverse "sailboats," most of which we set in motion ourselves. Isaiah said, "Woe unto them that decree unrighteous decrees." How many times have you emphatically made an "unrighteous" decree, such as, "It's going to be another one of those days!" We have decreed a thousand things that we did not want to happen but that have come to pass, and we have suffered the woeful consequences.

Often you may find yourself in a conversation that runs entirely to the negative side. Your friends may discuss the viruses that are going around, the economy, corporate downsizing, job insecurity, or gossip about other persons. And if there should be disagreement with the company about new work rules, the cumulative acrimony may actually fill the atmosphere with poisons toxic to the system of the company in general, and of each of the employees in particular.

If you want to make the Truth work for you, you must take seriously this matter of word toxins. You must set a seal upon your lips and refuse to contribute even the smallest negative word to any conversation. If you can change the subject, do so. You might even come prepared to turn to some topics that will lend themselves to positive conversations. Otherwise, keep silent.

The words you speak are not simply throw-away items; they are the visible outshowing of the Universal Creative Process. Of course, words have no power *of themselves*: it is our *feelings* and *beliefs* that are the energizing power. We empower the words with this creative energy, either positive or negative, and they "go forth to accomplish that whereto they are sent." It is just not good sense to put into words something that you really do not want to see outformed in your life. It is like playing Russian roulette with the creative process.

Since we are verbal creatures, this is an awesome responsibility and not an easy task. It calls for much discipline on our part, who have been too easy on ourselves, too permissive about our speech. It calls for a new way of life, watching that we say what we really want to say—not what we are impetuously led to say from force of habit—and becoming aware of the feelings that trigger the words.

Generations of "let-it-all-hang-out" permissiveness have left us as a society with a legacy of profanity. Words of profanity, especially those of the four-letter variety, actually inject into the system of the user (and into the atmosphere of the planet) a high level of toxicity. Those who sincerely wish to achieve fully functioning lives, and a world fit to live in, will carefully try to erase all profanity from their speech. It not only misrepresents us, but it leads to poor communication.

I want to suggest that you embark on a program of *detoxification* of the poisonous effect of negative and profane words. You will especially need to take stock of the many negatives that are a part of your habit-patterns of speech. It is rather like taking a course in public speaking. (You may say that you are not interested in giving speeches in public, but that is not what I have in mind; I am thinking of words that are actually *thoughts* externalized, and thus in the "public domain.")

Now what are negative words? They are words that identify you with—*and as*—sickness, lack, inharmony, fear, hate, and evil. They are words that identify us with, and as, that which we really do not want to see manifest in our lives. Of course there are the obvious phrases that we have absorbed from the race consciousness, and which we unthinkingly repeat by habit, such as "My aching back"; "I could just die"; "That will be the end of me".

But consider some of the more subtle toxins, such as *only*: "I only make thus-and-so on my job." Back of the "only" qualification is generally a thought of limitation. You say you have *only* a dollar. But you *do* have a dollar! Don't dwell in *onlyness*. Give thanks for the inner flow of abundance.

There is the toxin of *but*. You may say, "I know my body temple has the unique capacity to heal itself, but . . .". It is a case of faith limited by this little word *but*. Another is *I'm afraid*: "I'm afraid there is not enough time." What is enough time? The only time is now. If you do what needs to be done in the now, there will always be sufficient time to do the things that need to be done by you. So what are you "afraid" of?

You might try an interesting experiment purely in your imagination. Picture yourself as always within earshot of a voice-activated recorder. All your conversations and off-hand comments are caught on tape. Replaying the tape, you will be amazed at the number of direct or implied negatives that are in your speech-flow.

Often you are being facetious, or expressing light-hearted cynicism. But remember: the subconscious mind can't take a joke. It accepts your words as orders, which it works tirelessly to fill, even though you didn't mean any of it.

I have often wondered what might happen in our country if everyone would fast from negative words (and profanity) for one whole day—like a fast on a High Holy Day. For one day people would speak only if they had something important to say and could say it positively. I believe the vibrations of the ethers would be charged with positive energy. Hospitals would record a marked increase in recovery rates. Offices and shops would experience an upsurge of harmony and productivity. The nation's economy would begin a marked turnaround.

There are those who will say, "No way—it could never happen." This is a good example of the negative clichés we would be fasting from. One thing is certain: your personal fast from negative words would change the vibrational patterns that influence your life in a way that some would call miraculous.

PosiTrend:

*As co-creator, I am the conduit
through which the Creation unfolds.*

*My words are life and they are spirit
and they accomplish that
whereto they are sent.*

*I speak only those words
that I want to see outformed in my life.*

negatrend

➤ "The morality of expediency" "Everyone is doing it" "The delusion of living by the Ten Commandments" The practice of the absence of God.

More time is often spent in trying to get a good image than in improving the product or in eliminating the character defects in the person.

The Word Is *Integrity*

At the moment of this writing, in the news is the story of yet another scandal coming out of Washington. Politicians scurry about to find safe positions from which they "view with alarm." And the clergy preach sermons about the need to get "back to God." I am not sure I know what they mean by this. If it means returning to "moralistic hellfire preaching" and a steady stream of pious clichés, I am not too enthusiastic. But if the "back to God" movement means a renewed effort to improve general conduct and to change character, and also to modify consciousness, then I say "Amen" to that! What is needed is a deeper consciousness of the omnipresence of God, a perception of God as Principle, unchanging, ever active.

Unfortunately, religious institutions are too often into absolution instead of transformation. As does the business world, they deal in image-making. Someone has said, "It is good to be seen going to church, especially to the correct one," with the emphasis on a sought-after reputation, even if little is done to change character or enrich consciousness.

A few years ago, the director of creative projects at NBC News told a group of advertising people that the worst word ever coined by advertising folk was *image*. He said that substance and truth are the important things, even if the picture presented is not pleasant. But merchants and public figures strive unceasingly to protect or improve their image. An image must be a true reflection, or it is a phoney. Image is reputation, which is nothing more than what people have been trained and conditioned to think about an individual or a product or an organization. More time is often spent in trying to get a good image, to build a good reputation, than in improving the product or in eliminating the defects of character in the person.

Actually, this emphasis on image is the most important clue to the state of modern morality. The word *morals* comes from the Latin *mores*, which means "custom," or accepted rightness. Social morality is based on the mores of the time. In Puritan America it was immoral and illegal to kiss one's spouse in front of one's own house. Because a thing becomes right or wrong by the way it is currently viewed, we rarely have virtue and respectability at the same

time. To be respectable, it may be that we have to follow the accepted patterns of the times. We tend to
believe that the most important thing is *getting there*,
with no serious thought about *how* we get there or of
earning the right to be there.

In trying to understand the behavior of people at
the top, we use the phrase "the morality of expediency." The fact that "everyone is doing it" somehow renders it right and acceptable; but how far can
we go in this direction? The important thing for us
should be not what is being done, but rather "What
is the best one can do?" The Hindus say that it is not
a matter of being superior to other people but of being superior to your former self.

There are those who say they realize the need for
moral standards, but they do not need religion or the
church, for they just live by the Ten Commandments
and let their conscience be their guide. This may
often be a subtle cover-up of consciousness. For how
many of these "live-by-the-Ten-Commandments"
people could recite the Decalogue—even two or three
of the commandments—let alone really abide by
them?

It is simplistic to say that all one needs is the Ten
Commandments. Of course, you may be surprised
at the practical wisdom in the commandments if you
take the time to break them down to their underlying meaning. This is what I have attempted in my
book *Metamorality* (originally titled *How to Break the
Ten Commandments*). Strangely, the idea of breaking the commandments was offensive to the sensibil-

ities of even hardened editors. I have come to realize that people seem to need a facade of symbolic religion.

Perhaps we need an eleventh commandment: "Do not lie to yourself about what you really believe." This could begin a new morality. It reminds me of the vagrant who stood up in church at a testimonial meeting and said, "I know I ain't what I oughta be. In my time I have swore and smoked and been drunk, and I haven't been above finding a few things before they were lost. But I am here to tell you—I ain't never lost my religion!"

But what *is* religion? Is it a set of tenets that you once accepted on what the little boy calls "confusion of faith"? Is it a church or synagogue you belong to and perhaps stay away from? Or is it a vocabulary of clichés, such as "living by the Ten Commandments"?

The Ten Commandments deal with one thing: *integrity*. It is interesting that this word comes from the same root as the word *religion*. *Integrity* means "whole, undivided, unity"; *religion* means "to bind together into one." The word is *integrity*! And this is what the Ten Commandments are about. However, this doesn't come through when they are dealt with in a crystallized sense. We must break through the veneer of theological sentimentality and piety to discover the realistic spiritual laws involved. (This is what my book purports to do; and modestly, I feel that it is an important work.)

In this matter of conscience: *can* your conscience be your guide? The patriots of warring nations follow their consciences into conflict, even though they are antithetical. Conscience is an acquired sense of right and wrong. It is not necessarily divine guidance. One who has been instructed in honesty and fair play as the correct way of getting along with people may feel pangs of conscience if he fails to live up to them, but a society can train its youth to feel conscience-stricken if they do not bring home an enemy's head on a pole.

The great need is to find a lofty spiritual awareness and to let this express through our consciousness. Then we can let our Truth-directed conscience be our guide. The "good life" is not measured by the degree to which we conform to outer codes and systems, but by the degree to which we know ourselves and give expression to the divine dimension of our nature, living by what Thornton Wilder calls "the incredible standard of excellence."

If you measure your work or your conduct by that of another, you have taken your attention off the divine image in which you were created. If you conform to standards of thinking and living set by human practices of the world, you fail to live up to the best that is within you. You may be of your own time, but you are out of time as far as the divine process is concerned. What really counts in the individual life is not what is being done this season, but what is the very best that one can do.

In a book of some years ago by Carlyle Marney, there is an interesting reference to General Dean, who was captured by the Chinese–North Korean forces. They told General Dean that he had five minutes in which to write a letter home to his family. He assumed he was going to be taken out and shot. What would be your message to an only son at such a time? Marney says that he saw the letter General Dean wrote. It consisted of eight or nine lines. Down in the middle of it there was this one sentence: "Tell Bill the word is *integrity.*" The author then goes on to comment that it is significant that he did not write, "Tell Bill the word is *popularity* or *happiness,* or *success at all costs.*" No! The word is *integrity.*

A common cliché is, "Honesty is the best policy." But honesty that is simply a policy could quite conceivably lapse. Honesty is a principle of right action that comes from integrity, a sure integration of the individual with God. The child needs to be taught what true integrity is by the example of his or her adult models: parents, teachers, and religious, political, and business leaders. Children are given continual demonstrations of dishonesty that are often judged on the basis of "Did he get caught?" When a parent doesn't want to get involved with a salesman at the door and instructs a child to "Tell the man mother is not home," that child receives a dramatic lesson that integrity may be selective.

In school the teacher has an obligation to help the children understand that students who cheat on an examination may pass the test, but that the purpose of the test is not to limit them, but to enrich them. By cheating they deny themselves the enrichment that the course was intended to bring, but which never can be theirs so long as they fail to keep the law of integrity.

True integrity means meeting life as a mature spiritual being, realizing the importance of living within the bounds of spiritual principle—knowing that even if you can get away with some dishonesty, you can never get away *from* it, for under the law of compensation, you must always "pay the piper."

Here is an experience that can happen to anyone. Suppose when paying your check in a restaurant, you suddenly realize that the cashier has given you too much change. What to do? If your life is focused on receiving, you might rationalize that it is a divine out-working, a repayment for all those times when you have been short-changed. And after all, who would know? But if you know the Cosmic Law, you know that you can never get something for nothing. The decision is easy. Out of your giving consciousness you call it to the cashier's attention immediately.

You may recall a news item a few years ago about a man who came upon a bag that had fallen unnoticed out of a Brink's armored truck. The bag contained half a million dollars in small-denomination bills, unmarked and untraceable. Without hesitation he called the authorities and turned it in. He tells how his life was made miserable for months by people who asked him angrily, "Why did you turn it in?" They seemed to be saying, "We the underprivileged of society had this one chance of getting back. But you blew it. No one would ever have known!" His steady reply: "But *I* would know." He had his integrity intact, which meant more to him than any instant fortune.

Integrity is a commitment to spiritual law. Institutional religion puts chief emphasis on being good. Obviously it is a judgment made by the clergy on the basis of scriptural law. But the same scriptural law found Jesus lacking, and crucified him. Someone once knelt down before Jesus, saying, "Good Master . . ." But Jesus quickly demurred, saying, "Why callest thou me good? None is good save God."

Theological goodness means keeping the commandments, going to services, fulfilling various religious codes. Obviously this leaves many unanswered questions. For example, a pillar of religion has a tragic health crisis and people cry out, "How could such a good religious person suffer so?" The answer: "Because they are not good enough." Life is consciousness. Thus in a metamoral sense, goodness is not just concerned with conduct, or even with character, but with *consciousness*—the level of thinking and feeling. A person may have done nothing "bad"; but in their worry or negative talk about it, they are giving their support to the condition. They lose their integrity, thus breaking spiritual law.

The great Truth that Jesus taught is that we are spiritual beings, no matter how we frustrate this inherency; that the world is a spiritual world, no matter how the innate goodness is concealed; and that the underlying, controlling force is spiritual law, no matter what appearances may indicate. Remember that Jesus said, "Judge not according to appearances, but judge righteous judgment." Righteous judgment is seeing with the single eye. It is seeing with a spiritual perception that reflects oneness with God-Mind.

We need to work on becoming single-eyed to the Truth. Prepare yourself for every foray into the world. Don't let the world turn the lights on in you; turn the focused spotlight of your spiritual insight onto the world. Don't let people or events determine how you are going to act or react. Let your light shine!

Every morning of your life take time to become centered in the flow of divine action. You can always release the light and guidance and strength with which to meet the changing conditions that may come. You can, if you will. It is more than just making the decision in church on Sunday or when you are in prayer or meditation. There's a tendency to make the decision when you are involved in the big difficulties of life; but the big things, the crises and conflicts, will always be determined by the state of consciousness in which they find you.

In other words, the big game at Madison Square Garden isn't just played at that particular moment. It is played day after day in practice—the constant process of mental and physical conditioning, working for self-control and speed and coordination. Jesus walked out of the tomb to prove his mastery over life. But the consciousness to do this was not acquired in the three days in the tomb; it was achieved during the whole thirty-three years of his life—in self-denial and discipline.

The study of the new insight into Truth deals with the idea that there is an omnipresence of divine law, and that where we are, no matter what the needs, we are in the flow of the activity of Spirit. Our work is to practice the Presence, which means to keep consciously in the flow, to experience guidance and life and love. We must change the habit of the practice of the *absence* of God, which we do whenever we stew and fret; whenever we dwell on mistakes or harbor hurts from mistreatment; in short, when we lose our integrity. The goal for us all is to practice the Presence of God. Begin by affirming, "There is only one Presence and one Power: God the good, omnipotent." There can be no separation. You and the Father are one, not two. Go forth into every day in this consciousness.

The Psalmist says, "Thou wilt keep him in perfect peace, whose mind is stayed on thee." This is integrity—keeping the mind focused on the "still point" at the center of your being. When you stray from that focus, you open the door to all manner of ills.

Consider this illustration: When last you entered a motion picture theater, you were confronted with an aisle, which is actually a runway, about five feet wide. You walked confidently down this aisle-runway with no consideration of the hazards of falling off. To make it more impressive let us imagine raising the aisle to the height of the stage. Now you can get the sense of a runway. You would probably walk down it, but now you would be more careful.

But suppose we elevate this same runway to a height of 1,000 feet and suspend it between the towers of the World Trade Center. Now would you walk the runway? I doubt very much if you would.

Why not? It is the same runway and the same width as the aisle down which you walked confidently. But now you become preoccupied with the space around the runway and the possibility of falling off. The reason the high-beam construction worker does his work so fearlessly is that he is confident of his ability and he does not borrow trouble by worrying about falling. And he never does. His mind is stayed on the stability of the beam. The word is *integrity*.

There is a tendency to focus on the fear of consequences. "What if I lose my job?" "What if there is not enough money to meet my obligations?" By the law of consciousness, if you are locked into a fear consciousness, you will become vulnerable to the very thing you fear. So the positive way is to begin setting up a series of positive sequences of thought that will lead to positive consequences.

I like the wisdom of Marcus Aurelius: "Let others pray not to lose their children, let me pray not to fear losing them." The same with your job, your relationship, etc. Hold fast to your integrity.

Some years ago, a businessman came to me for counseling. He was terribly depressed. He outlined a long list of problems, and he was a little annoyed because I didn't sympathize with him. I told him that he was a spiritual being, with the mind of the Infinite in focus as him, and in him there was a solution for every problem, and the guidance to work it out. I challenged him to help himself by thinking and speaking constructively. He looked at me for a moment, and then said, "Oh, you New Age people are all alike!

You hate to face facts!" Emerson says, "For what is prayer but the contemplation of the facts of life from the highest point of view."

Paul points out that we "see in part." When the appearances indicate lack or illness, if we get centered within, we will catch the vision of wholeness. You may have been brooding over an inadequacy or a sense of inferiority. You may say, "I might as well face the fact that I am inferior." In that moment you are losing your integrity.

The Truth is, you are not really inferior. Nor are you ever superior. You are simply you. You are a divine original. You are wonderful (full of wonder). The need is not to change yourself—but to change your self-image.

We must learn to tell the Truth about ourselves and our experiences. By this I mean to look beyond appearances and identify with the whole, otherwise we will be only half-living and half-using the potentialities of our being. When we tell the Truth we get in tune with the Universal Creative Flow, and amazing things begin to unfold.

In your work you may be promoted to a position for which you have no previous experience. You may be flattered at the confidence the management has in you, but you have doubts about your ability and fears that you may fail. You may feel helpless in a situation that seems hopeless. But remember, the word is *integrity*. The facts may cry out that with your inexperience, you can't possibly do the job. What about the eternally true fact of divine wisdom? And what about the Truth? Hold fast to your integrity. You might affirm: "God is in charge of this situation, and I am here only as a channel. God has a way, and I will draw to me both the ideas and the people by which the job can be accomplished easily and effectively."

When you succeed in solving the problem (and you will succeed), tell the Truth. In humility acknowledge that it was "not by might, nor by power, but by my Spirit." The integrity of the Universe is ever your support. When you really believe in the integrity of the Universe, integrity becomes the leading jewel in your crown. With your trust in the awareness of the creative flow, you will be secure and confident in every situation. In all that pertains to your life, THE WORD IS INTEGRITY.

PosiTrend:

Let people everywhere
become completely integrated persons
expressing integrity
individually and collectively.

I participate joyously
in this global unfoldment.

➤ The history of civilization is a saga of violence, and the sad trend is that America has become the most violent society in the world.

In business dealings and in arbitration sessions, the trend is toward resistant and aggressive behavior, and the widespread use of profanity that makes for poor communication and renunciation of our heritage of gentleness.

A Heritage
of Gentleness

One of the saddening trends in America is the increasing use of violence in relationships. Few people are aware of the extent to which violence has proliferated in our society. Here is a startling statistic: In 1992, handguns were used in the murders of 33 people in Britain, 36 in Switzerland, 218 in Canada, 13 in Australia, 60 in Japan, *and 13,220 in the United States*. Can you grasp the enormity of these figures? We have become by far the most violent society in all the world. We could coin a word to describe this almost unique American breed of violence: *pistolence*.

Thus in the count-up to the Millennium here is a trend that needs to be reversed. The spiritual counterpart to violence is gentleness, which is a fundamental of the teachings of Jesus—needless to say, one that has been sadly neglected.

Emerson cites the report of Cavendish to Lord Hunsdon in 1588 on his return from a voyage around the world. It tells of his many escapades and includes the shocking statement, "All the villages and towns that I ever landed at, I burned and spoiled." And the pious Cavendish report begins with the amazing statement, "It hath pleased Almighty God."

Failing to grasp the fundamentals of love and non-resistance and the heritage of gentleness, the church has acquiesced in and even given support to some of the world's most vicious wars. Without a doubt, if Jesus' teachings were understood and practiced, we would see an end to all war and all conflict between nations and factions and classes. More than this, we would take a giant step toward eliminating the cause of illness.

The lesson of history is clear: "Gentleness is able to accomplish what violence cannot." But it is a vital lesson that humankind has failed to learn, because of the preoccupation with guns and bombs and armed might. The number of guns in the hands of Americans of all ages is beyond belief, and a new handgun is produced every 20 seconds. What is this "thing" about guns?

But it need not continue unabated. We can change. Yes, the lessons of history are quite clear. Napoleon, after setting the world on fire with the most violent of emotions, came finally to realize the futility of it all. In exile, reflecting on the whole pattern of his experience, he said, "The more I study the world, the more I am convinced of the inability of brute force to create anything durable." We might say, "Thanks a lot! *Now* you tell us—after you have turned the world upside down!"

What a different world there might have been if the Napoleons and Hitlers and Genghis Khans of history had found the light early in life. David, the shepherd king of Israel, who worked out his aggressions a little earlier and was able to salvage a period of greatness for his people, said in one of his singing soliloquys, "The Lord is my rock and my fortress. . . . In him will I trust. . . . Thou savest me from violence, and thy *gentle*ness hath made me great."

The word *gentle* is defined as "mild, kindly, amiable—not severe or violent." And it has synonyms, such as *courteous, tender, compassionate, considerate, tolerant, smooth, calm*—with the added connotation of *(a person of) honorable birth.*

At one time the words *gentleman* and *gentlewoman* had rich meaning, suggesting one of character, of breeding, of poise and dignity—one who had accepted the "noblesse oblige" that goes with culture. We find this in Shakespeare when he says, "We must be gentle now that we are gentlemen."

It is sad to see how this quality has been eroded in the past three decades by the tendency to "let it all hang out," to "tell it like it is," and "to be honest"

(which usually means to be negative, perhaps un-
couth, and often to intersperse the conversation with
a plethora of four-letter words). I am shocked at what
passes for language in places where people "hang
out," where it seems as if some people can't put two
words together without a word of vulgar profanity.
It is not that I am a prude or that I am making a
moral judgment. It is simply that it is poor communication, a renunciation of our heritage of gentleness.

Homo sapiens is innately a gentle creature, whose
crowning grace down through the ages has not been
brute strength but his divine potential. The kind of
behavior we see so much of in modern times, and
which has been accepted as normal, prevents us from
really knowing ourselves, and thus from releasing
our inner powers. Thus, expressing ourselves from
a low rung of our human experience, there is little
left for us but to meet life with willpower and aggressiveness.

Any actions or words that express other than true
gentleness are a frustration of the flow of life in us.
This frustration gives rise to what I call "mental
cholesterol," which blocks the flow of health and
abundance in our lives.

It is unfortunate that we have tended to think
of gentleness and meekness as signs of weakness.
Meekness is one of the cornerstone concepts of Jesus that have been widely misunderstood. "Blessed
are the meek for they shall inherit the earth": this
Beatitude has rarely been given a decent hearing, be-

cause to human sense it doesn't make good sense. Everyone knows that it is the strong, the assertive, and the aggressive who inherit the earth and gather up the spoils. If he had said, "Blessed are the meek for they shall inherit heaven," it might be more acceptable. The problem is we have a misunderstanding of "meekness"; and it has been our great loss, for in this Beatitude Jesus gives one of the great keys to power and achievement.

The Greek word *praeis*, which we translate into "meek," really means "tame"—as opposed to being wild or unrestrained. It refers to harnessing and mobilizing one's powers. Certainly it suggests a manner of reserve and control, of poise and serenity. However, it is not weakness but strength, for all the inner powers are harnessed in reserve—not dissipated in bluster and show.

The Niagara River has poured over the Niagara Falls for eons. Scientists found a way to harness energy from the Falls through great hydroelectric plants that turned the power of the Falls into electric energy. So today as you see the high-tension wires running out in all directions from the hydroelectric plants of Niagara Falls, you could say that the "meekness" of the Niagara River has inherited the earth. The oriental adage says, "Meekness compels God Himself." This doesn't mean surrendering fearfully to people, but surrendering to the creative flow.

The best conductor of electricity is the substance

that is least resistant to the flow of current, and the best conductor of divine power is the person who is nonresistant to its flow.

It is interesting that the French translation of the Bible renders the Beatitude "Blessed are the meek" as "Blessed are the debonair." This gives a whole new dimension of meaning. The word *debonair* means "of pleasant manner, courteous, gracious, charming, and carefree." This suggests a contemporary word from the swinging culture: *cool*— "Blessed are the cool," who have it all together. When you get it all together, and have yourself in harness, you don't have to get your way through bluster and show. You can be "cool," and this coolness projects a positive power that goes much further in a relationship or experience than any amount of force or assertiveness or aggressiveness.

The gentle person has a lot of give in him. He has the capacity to give way. He is big enough so that he doesn't have to belittle. He doesn't have to put people down, to undercut them or underbid them. He doesn't have to hammer away in an argument for the "principle of the thing." One who is "cool" knows that the *true* principle of the thing is a supportive process, and so he can easily give in for the sake of harmony.

A person often says, "I am fighting for my good name." But if you have a good name, it needs no defense. To fight for it is to reveal your insecurity and your self-doubts. When someone makes a slur against you or impugns your character, if you are "cool" you can, instead of lashing out in defense, quietly say to yourself, "It's interesting that they feel that way. I wonder what is disturbing them?"

In other words, it is not a question of why they say that about me, but about why I am disturbed by what they say. One who is "cool" knows when to step back, to give way, when going on might simply be willfulness. They do not borrow trouble by insisting on their rights or fighting for their freedom. They know that the only truly free person is one who keeps his heart free from hatred and conflict.

When we live in a large city, we encounter much heavy traffic—traffic of all kinds—in work relationships, in social situations, in family involvements, and of course in driving in the streets and highways. If everyone insisted on their rights, there would be little hope of harmony. Any counselor or arbiter knows that there are times when it is not all black or white, right or wrong. God is on both sides of the bargaining table, in both persons engaged in a dispute.

In all such conflicts, courtesy and generosity and gentleness are not just "Sunday School clichés." They are practical alternatives to chaos. Blessed are the meek—the person who has it all together and is strong enough so that he can step back, when pressing forward to win the argument might lead to losing his inner peace.

Imagine four cars at a busy traffic intersection where the traffic light has broken down. By law each one has the right of way for each is on the right of another car. They are honking and wildly gesticulating in furious impatience. The result: deadlock, leading to a massive gridlock. They all have the right of way, and all must yield. But who? And to whom?

A few years ago a city planner remarked that some day all the cars will come into the city and there will be a traffic jam of such monumental proportions, that it would be decided that the only solution would be to cover the cars all over and pave new roads.

We may encounter a situation like this in human relations, in business dealings, in various types of arbitration sessions. One who does not understand the dynamics of gentleness may assume that to give way or step back would be a sign of weakness. But the opposite is true. The one who cannot bring himself to give way is the one who is weak, because he does not trust himself. He does not believe in the cosmic law that no one can keep his good from him, and that by giving way he will open the way to a new flow of good far surpassing the time or substance or even dignity he may feel he has lost.

I read a story about a cab company that features the slogan "Wave them through and watch them smile." It is stamped in bright letters on the driver's clipboard, reminding him to be "cool," courteous, and gentle. *Wave them through*—and when the other person breaks into a smile (he can't help himself) there will be a chain reaction set off. The other person will find himself feeling, "Now wasn't that a nice thing for him to do?" He will wave back and smile as he goes on his way in a whole consciousness. The next thing you know he will be waving someone else through, and someone else will smile. And each one will leave a mile of smiles behind him. The whole consciousness of the city will reflect a higher vibration that day.

The important thing is not who is influenced by the wave of your hand, by your gentleness of spirit, but rather what it does to you in the waving. Your gentleness will, by cosmic law, lead to all that will make for a good day for you.

We have thought that dynamic people are those who are aggressive, domineering, and flamboyant—those who thunder through life. But the truly dynamic people are not noisy. They are meek in the sense of having it all together, their powers in control. They fulfill the word of the poet, "When you are the anvil, bear. . . . When you are the hammer, strike."

They can speak with authority, and take decisive action with power and conviction. But they don't beat the drum! Instead of thundering, they use the lightning of ideas! Instead of battering doors, they use a key! Instead of cursing the darkness, they turn on the light!

It could be said that there is a hard way and an easy way to do everything—and people, in human consciousness, have often tended to do things the hard way: the way of power and force and influence. Here and there, however, someone has achieved immortality by doing something the easy way.

Some years ago in New York Harbor there was a sunken gunboat that posed a problem to East River riverboat traffic. Authorities offered a large sum of money to anyone who could raise the boat and tow it out into deep water. Many salvage companies tried and failed. The dead weight broke all the cables each time an attempt was made to raise the iron vessel.

Then along came a "cool" young man who did it with ease. How? He floated several sand barges into position and lashed them to the sunken boat at the lowest point of the tide. He didn't try to raise the boat with derricks. He simply waited for the tide to come in. The tide raised the floating barges, which easily lifted the gunboat out of the muddy bed. Then he let the tide on its outward flow move the barges gently out to sea, where he dropped the boat into the deep water.

Saint Francis DeSales said, "Nothing is as strong as gentleness; and nothing is as gentle as true strength."

Note, we are not talking about weakness or passivity or indolence or procrastination. We are talking about life that is together, talents focused, powers harnessed, and manner "cool."

I once had an interesting conversation with a friend who is wealthy and successful. He says that young people come to him asking him to use his influence to get them a promotion or a better job. He says he is amazed by the attitude that prompts such requests. He says he feels like telling them that the fact that they spend time and thought campaigning for another position proves that they may not be worthy even of the one they now hold. That might be a shock to one who follows the "know-what-you-want-and-reach-out-and-get-it" philosophy of success.

This man, who started out as an office boy, says that in all his years he has never asked for a raise or promotion, or even thought about it. He had but one thought: how to make his company tops in its field. He wanted to see it spread its influence to every corner of the world. And, he says, "I have simply been given the opportunity to make my vision come true. And the company to which I have given my life has given it back to me a hundred times richer than my own selfish thought and aggressive planning could possibly have made it."

Emerson says it well: "The average run of persons fret and worry themselves into nameless graves, while here and there a great gentle soul forgets himself into immortality."

What all this means is that your fortune, your good, your success and achievement in life begin with you. No one can keep them from you. No one can really stand in your way. If you have enemies, *you* are your own worst enemy by the very fact of your enmity. You may want to lash out and set things and people right. But the gentle way is to be "cool" and see them rightly.

In our quest for world peace, perhaps it is time to be nationally "debonair," "cool," and controlled. It may be important to carry the "big stick," as Theodore Roosevelt urged. But he also emphasized the need to "speak softly." Then we will not stew about who is the most powerful nation. We will seek to be the most humane, the most loving, the most gentle.

E. Stanley Jones, a renowned Christian missionary, tells of seeing a little frail flower growing in the vast ruins of ancient Babylon. He wondered how this little flower, so frail that he coud crush it in his fingers, could have survived while this vast empire founded on military might had perished. He realized it was because the flower obeyed the laws of God written within itself. It lived. The empire disobeyed those laws. It perished. The flower followed the ways of nature's gentleness—but the nation perished by its own militarist doctrine.

To all the violence and conflicts in the world, gentleness is a creative alternative. It is not just a Sunday School ideal that we espouse one day a week. It is a matter of understanding that each of us has a heritage of gentleness. It is the way you really are. And when you get it all together, you find that suddenly you have the "secret" power that will go before you and make safe, easy, and successful your way. Gentleness is a very scientific, a very wonderful, and a very meaningful way to approach life. It is something that we all would do well to give focus to as we enter the gate into the golden years of the New Millennium.

PosiTrend:

I renounce all thoughts and acts of violence.

I walk and work in ways of gentleness.
I do not insist on my rights
or fight for my freedom
for I know that the only truly free person
is one who keeps his heart
free from hatred and conflict.

My gentleness is not weakness
but strength.

I take decisive action
with power and conviction.

But I don't beat the drum!

Instead of thundering
I use the lightning of ideas!

Instead of battering doors
I use a key!

Instead of cursing the darkness
I turn on the light!

negatrend

➤ You cannot be a "fully functioning" person if you are enslaved by crutches and excessive dependencies. Commit yourself to the path of Truth; you have nothing to lose but your chains. Among the negatrends that prevail in this premillennial inventory, the problems of drugs and alcohol and cigarettes are high on the list of negative trends that call for resolution.

Victory over Excessive Dependencies

We have become a nation of exteriorly oriented people, obsessed with the idea that we can solve our problems or cure our ills or pep us up or calm us down or put us to sleep or keep us awake only with substances administered through the mouth. This whole syndrome is abetted by skillfully created commercials selling everything from "fast relief for indigestion," to helping you cope with stress. The message that these commercials impress on the subconscious mind is: "You can't do anything by yourself—so just put your trust in this formula."

If we would listen more to our bodies and the creative energy that flows through them, and less to the appeal of quick-relief formulas, we would clearly know that it is never really necessary to take the cocktail to relax us, the cigarette to relieve the tension, or the cup of coffee to get us going. Every time you give in to the addiction, you are taking one more step in losing control of your life. And when you lean on anything other than the strength of the Almighty, you lose something of your self-respect.

This is not making a judgment on what you do in your life. You are a free creature. I am merely concerned that you take charge of your life and maintain your hold on the reins perpetually. It is sad to see how many are living a life in chains, due to their addictions and to the frustrations of their greater potential.

Richard Rumbold once said, "I never could believe that providence had sent a few persons into the world, ready, booted, and spurred to ride—and millions ready, saddled, and bridled to be ridden." Of course he was addressing social injustice. But following his line of reasoning we could say that it is inconceivable that any one of us was intended to be ridden by the wild horses of mind or emotions, or condemned to go through life on crutches of excessive dependency.

Most of us have been conditioned to a feeling of personal inadequacy by the belief that we are born into life as empty creatures who must go forth into the world to become defined and fulfilled. We begin life empty of love, of wisdom, of support. And so we go forth in life carrying little begging bowls, begging for love from our parents, begging for career success from the marketplace, begging for learning from our schools, begging for religious values from our churches, and begging for general acceptance from the people we live with.

And unless something happens within us that reveals to us our uniqueness, and our personal relationship with the inner flow, we increasingly look for sure harbors, snug retreats, strong arms, and outer sources of love and guidance. And we reach for all kinds of synthetic means of support.

A helpful technique for dealing with excessive dependencies is the "support group" concept that was popularized by Alcoholics Anonymous. Excessively dependent persons come together and share their common needs—and give group support for common weaknesses.

Taking their cue from A.A., scores of support groups have evolved as a means of enabling searchers for help and overcoming to break the chains of excessive dependency: Over-Eaters Anonymous and Gamblers Anonymous are just two such.

It is important to recognize that the support group must always be the *means* toward the end of growth and freedom—not the end in itself. Every person is a spiritual being, a whole creature, with the potential to become a fully functioning person.

It is possible to become excessively dependent on the support group! This would be to give up one dependency for another. A creative alternative is the "support group of one," which is to become *within*-dependent.

How great is the need to discover that "He that is within me is greater than he that is within the world" and to know that within every person is the potential to meet and overcome any situation or experience without leaning on people or resorting to stimulants!

Now, let's not oversimplify the process of achieving victory over an excessive dependency. It will not "just happen" to you without effort. You will have to grow, to dig a little deeper to release the inner strength to overcome the need. But then growth is what life is all about.

Once a dependency has become excessive, it becomes rigidly entrenched, so that it becomes difficult to even think about giving up this "crutch." The first step is to admit to yourself that it *is* a crutch—and that it is based on feelings of inadequacy. Then you are ready for the Truth that can set you free: the realization that although you have frustrated your divine potential, within you is the power and sufficiency to meet things with courage and self-reliance.

If you take an honest inventory of your life, you may note that you are too easy on yourself; you may tend to rationalize your weaknesses. For instance, some persons carelessly eat themselves into awkward physical proportions and dubious health by saying, "I enjoy eating; I am a free creature. I can do what I want." Yet within yourself, you know that you are *not* free: you are a slave to your appetite. Freedom comes with restraint, when you let go your crutches.

As a young man I was fond of distance running. Long before the jogging craze, I used to run an average of 20 miles a week, running the mile and two-mile on the college track team. In the off-season I ran various road races, including the marathon. So I know from personal experience that a distance runner is often tempted to give up from exhaustion in the early stages of a race. The body struggles to assert its mastery over you.

But the experienced runner wages a tussle and presses past the point of fatigue. I discovered long years ago that if you concentrate your attention not on how tired you are becoming, but upon the cosmic flow of limitless energy within, in a magic moment of awareness you may experience what is called "second wind," whereupon new strength is amazingly released.

Discipline and restraint do not "just happen" but are the result of practice. Like stretching—always try to go a little further beyond the point of weakness, beyond the tendency to lean on someone for help, beyond the compulsion to reach for the cigarette or the sweets. So occasionally pass up a meal when you want to control your weight but find that you are being ruled by the dinner bell. Take time to realize your inner support before you "run home to momma." Try reaching for God before reaching for the aspirin bottle; try a brief meditation before giving in to medication.

Understand, I am not moralizing. This is not a moral issue. I am not saying or even implying that drinking or smoking or gambling or overindulgence of any kind is sinful. The old-time religion didn't help matters by laying a burden of guilt on the person who was already loaded down with self-condemnation. Of course there may be hazards to your physical and mental health in these excesses, but that is another matter.

You can get rid of your crutches, but first you must be willing to change your way of thinking. You must let go the tendency to think of yourself as weak. You can never become the strong person you are capable of becoming if you keep telling yourself what a weak sister you are. There is no such thing as inherent weakness. What you so term is simply a subconscious idea of weakness that has become a bad mental habit.

Let go once and for all the self-limiting cliché "That's just the way I am. I have always been like that." If you really believe that, then you are wasting your time with this new insight in truth. You might reflect on the retort of the little boy when piously asked by the minister, "Who made you?" He said, "Well, to tell you the truth, I ain't done yet."

You can change, you can turn your life around; but first you must understand that it is *your* life and that the locus of control is always within *your consciousness*—not in other people or events or chemicals. Thought is always parent to the act. You have the power to control your thinking, to determine the thoughts that enter your mind. More than likely you have been starting with external facts, and thus you have created a repetition of facts of a similar nature.

For instance you have seen a weakness and you say, "It is a fact that I am weak." But you are weak because you have held in your mind the image of weakness! The statements "I am weak . . . I am confused . . . I am inadequate" are actually crutches themselves. You can break this negative cycle by reversing the way you think. Instead of starting with facts, start with Truth. "Judge not according to appearances." In other words, don't just react; respond from a cosmic perspective. For instance, don't wait to see what the day will bring. *You* bring to the day a positive state of mind and a happy expectation.

Concerning the effort to change or overcome, we often say, "The Spirit is willing but the flesh is weak." It is an excellent excuse for procrastination. It is a kind of twist on the cliché "The devil made me do it."

Take a good look at that statement, "The Spirit is willing." What it says is that it is the divine will or creative intention of the Universe. It is always God's will that you find freedom and self-reliance. In God you are whole and complete, and you are intended to be that in manifestation. "The flesh is weak" should mean that the human of you can no longer resist the inexorable urging of the Spirit.

Unfortunately we have accepted weakness as our starting point: "After all, I'm only human." But you are not *only* human. You are human and divine—and the divine is enclosed in the shell of the human. Like the egg in the nest, you must hatch out. And you can. "The Spirit is willing" means that God wants to be your strength, your overcoming. The whole Universe is willing and is your support: a support group of *One*.

Now, this habit or excessive dependency that you would like to alter: do you *really* want to change? Or do you think you "ought" to? Have your loved ones and friends been telling you that you should? Do you have the feeling that you are involved in some secret sin, and that overcoming might bring a kind of absolution? All of these are insufficient motivations to achieve overcoming. To put it simply, *"You gotta wanta."* You must want to make the overcoming for no other reason than that you are ready for the next logical step in your personal development.

Don't make the mistake of hoping or even praying that a miracle will occur for you, for that can be a "cop-out." The desire for a miraculous overcoming is merely an unwillingness to take charge of your own life. Emerson says, "What you will have, quoth God, pay for it and take it." As Henri Bergson says, "An intelligent being carries within him the wherewithal to surpass himself." That is the miracle! Within you is the unborn possibility of limitless life, and yours is the privilege of giving birth to it. And that is the miracle!

You can overcome. You can be free of your excessive dependencies. But you must be willing to pay the price, which means to do the work of changing your life by altering your thoughts. Get out of the business of looking for miracle demonstrations. "God can do no more for you than He can do through you." But the whole person that you are need never be dependent on anyone or anything. The key is *within-dependence*.

Make a commitment that you will undertake the "overcoming project"—that of finding release from enslavement to excessive dependencies. Let your mind reflect the possibility that you have the power in you to be more than you now are, the power to overcome, to stand alone, to be self-sufficient. Say to yourself, "I *can* get rid of this crutch, and I *will!*"

But don't stop there. You can't overcome by will-power. The key might actually be *"won't* power." When you are tempted to give in, to start worrying, to reach for the chemical support, say to yourself, "No! I have a choice—and I choose to be strong." It is not by force of *will*, but by *willingness*. "I will" still deals with something yet to be done, and procrastination may still set in. "I will" deals with tomorrow. How often we say, "I will start the diet tomorrow"; "I am going to give up smoking starting next Monday." "Mañana" projects are the most common in the world—and they rarely get off the launching pad.

Instead say, "I can, I will, I AM." In other words always follow the "I can" and "I will" statements with the affirmation, "I *am* what I want to be. I *am* whole, I *am* free—now!"

PosiTrend:

*God has given you Himself
as your resource.*

He does not bestow Himself occasionally.

*He is your steady eternal resource
and your help in every need.*

*There is no longer anything in you
that feels incomplete
or inferior or insecure.*

*Your whole being
is satisfied and fulfilled.*

*You are not dependent
on any limiting habit
for your security and satisfaction.*

*Your faith is in God
and you are free.*

You are equal to every situation.

*You do not need
material support or stimulants
for God is your strength.*

*You are happy in your own right
complete and perfect
in your own being
divine and whole right now!*

negatrend

➤ "At my age . . ." Anxiety about security of retirement programs. Age is made a preoccupation; we talk about it, plan for it, expect it, resist it, and try to cover it up.

Mid-life crisis; equating maturity with resignation and decline.

"Is this all there is?" "What am I doing with my life?" Too young to retire, but too old to get another job.

*En*tirement in
the Golden Age

It is interesting to note the important part that words play in our lives. Consider the word *whole*. Have you ever thought what it means to be whole? From the same root we get the words *hale*, *hearty*, and *heal*.

Paul says, "I know in part" (1 Cor. 13:12). He is concerned that in our self-image we tend to fragment ourselves and life. He says: "When the perfect comes, the imperfect will pass away" (1 Cor. 13:10). It is the key to spiritual healing: when you get the image of yourself as a whole creature, the frustrations of that wholeness will disappear as darkness fades before the coming of light.

For instance, you might see yourself as young or as old. In both cases, you may be seeing yourself in part. No matter what the years say, you are not young, and you are not old. You are simply *you*, and *you* are *whole*. If you can catch this simple concept, you will open a whole new world of possibilities for yourself.

You might think of the work that was your life and livelihood for so many years. Perhaps you have been "downsized" (translation: dismissed, laid off). Or you may have been forced into an unwelcome retirement. Or you may have retired according to your long-range financial plan. If you perceive these developments in your life in a fragmented sense, something vital is missing in your experience. Retirement is almost universally conceived of outside the context of life, instead of as an experience *in* life.

A young worker just entering the job market, right out of school, will probably get very much involved, with society's encouragement, in plans for retirement. A good retirement plan is often an inducement to work for a particular employer. Through the years "the plan" almost becomes an obsession—a place to retire to and the financial means to make it possible. Unfortunately, the plan rarely involves anything relative to the kind of life you will live.

Thus when the day of retirement comes, the world may close in upon you. One doctor says, "Retirement is the greatest shock the human system can sustain." This is because retirement is usually a compromise, a partial experience in life. Most often something vital is left out, leaving frustration and hopelessness. Unless it deals with you as a whole person, retirement becomes an altogether negative experience.

Most persons will face some kind of retirement in the millennium to come. What counts is how you deal with it. Do you react to the crisis in resignation? Or do you respond to this challenge of change in the spirit of adventure, looking at it as a new opportunity, as a period of expansion and the integration of powers?

There is a creative alternative: *entirement*. This is a key word in the theology of the Golden Age of the Third Millennium. It deals with the whole self in a whole Universe. It is turning from the partial experience that involves a breakup of life as you have known it. Instead of going into retirement, it is going into *entirement*, into the next step, which will have meaning and the promise of a new kind of fulfillment. *Entirement* is a new word, dealing with an extremely important activity of consciousness. Let's think about it!

Goethe, at age thirty, had a grave crisis. It threatened to destroy all possibilities for a happy or productive experience. However, with an enlightenment that the ancients called "a gift of the gods," he resolved to work out life no longer by halves, but in all its beauty and totality. We are not told the nature of his crisis, but we can witness the results of a life turned around. He went into *entirement*, and in the next fifty-three years he became a great philosopher, writer, and poet.

Goethe thus points up an important insight: *entirement* is not just for retired persons. He went into *entirement* when he was only thirty. It is relevant and appropriate for one coming out of school and making plans to embark upon a new career. It is the commitment to live life as a whole person in a whole Universe, to always be what Rollo May calls a fully functioning person.

In this age of enlightenment there are still far too few persons who realize that life is lived from within-out, and that no matter what one's experience may be, one contains within oneself the wherewithal to be more, do more, and have more. Most of us have been conditioned to believe that the pattern of experience is all set, that "It's just the way I am!" Thus we go through the years simply becoming a little older. In this fragmented approach to life we have been encouraged to settle for the lesser, simply because we are not often challenged to pursue the greater.

It is an indisputable scientific fact that every person, under average conditions of work and life, uses only a small part of their mental equipment. If we were able to challenge ourselves to work at even half our mental capacity, we could, according to Russian psychologist Vassily Davidoff, learn forty languages, memorize the largest encyclopedia from cover to cover, and complete the required courses of dozens of colleges. And this has nothing to do with age. Research at Columbia University refuted the common excuse that it is difficult to learn new things "at my age." They found that any person, no matter

what age, could learn such difficult studies as short-
hand or the Russian language, and that the only reason an older person has more difficulty is that he has
bought into age as an excuse.

Every young person starting out in life needs to be
challenged to go into *en*tirement, to "work out life
no longer by halves, but in all its beauty and totality."
We should say to that person: "Don't be satisfied
with half a life. Go for it all! Always press past the
points of fatigue or difficulty or limitation. Life is
a growth process. There is more in you, and more
in life for you. Keep reaching for that more, and
keep the commitment to release your imprisoned
splendor."

One of the fundamentals of this new insight of
Truth for the Golden Age is that you are a spiritual
being. Do you know what this means? It means that
you are a whole creature, even if you see yourself in
part, and live half a life. It also means that the whole
of God is present in its entirety in you at all times,
even if you are locked into a concept of God "up
there" somewhere to whom you must appeal for bet-
terment and from whom life's blessings may be doled
out according to whim.

To go into *en*tirement is to change your attitudes
and expectations of yourself. It is to begin dealing
with yourself as if you were always on the verge of
great good. It is to get the feeling that the whole
Universe is breaking through to you, and that unborn
creative ideas are always awaiting birth in your mind.

It is good, occasionally, to go over all the things you

do, from shaving to cooking, from selling to managing, listening to new ideas, new directions, new methods. We tend to live too much on the surface, moving through life like water-striders skittering along on the surface of a lake. Living fully is getting in tune with inner rhythms, listening to your own inner guidance. As Montaigne says: "Put your ear close by yourself, and hold your breath and listen."

We seem to have a human disposition to downgrade ourselves. Certainly outstanding people come forth and reveal great inner powers. They win the races, scale the mountains, compose the music, build the cathedrals, and invent the machines. But we have downgraded ourselves by thinking that the Lincolns, the Gandhis, and the Einsteins were people quite different from the rest of us. The truth is, these people did great things not because of a special connection with the source, but rather by *specializing* the connection with the creative mind potential that is within everyone. This is not to say that anyone can become a Michelangelo or a Shakespeare or a Schweitzer. We wouldn't want to (or shouldn't). It is much better to be a first-rate *you* than a second-rate Picasso or Pavarotti. Our need is to keep the inner connection and then to fulfill our uniqueness.

To live a life of *entirement*, one needs to have a good perspective of what we call "aging," in terms of the continuity of life. The generally accepted concept of aging arises from identifying ourselves as physical bodies, birthing, growing, maturing, aging, and eventually decaying and dying. The cliché is,

"We all have to go sometime." One should ask, *"Go where?"* The keynote of life is growth. It might be better to say, "We all *grow* sometime. Why postpone it for some future eternity?" The truth is, you don't grow old. When you stop growing, you are old.

Somehow, in America, we have developed a distorted attitude toward aging and the aged. For this reason we have a great fear of growing old and being cast aside as unimportant. To be retired is almost something to be ashamed of.

Aging is not something that *happens to you.* It is something *you are doing.* It is an attitude that suggests a fragmentation of the whole person. The need is to stop aging and start "youthing." *Youthing* refers to a way of thinking and living. This does not imply immaturity, nor is it a frantic effort to recapture the years of your youth. There is no need to do this. You are where you are, and that is good.

What we need to realize is that many who try so hard to keep up with the changing fads and youthful physiques of young people are actually preoccupied with a morbid fear of age. Thus they are "aging." We need often to make a renewed commitment to *entirement,* to recapture the enthusiasm and curiosity and zest for life of the youth, which is to let the creative flow unfold in us regardless of our years. This is *youthing.* The youthing process has little to do with appearances, but more to do with an open-mindedness that is free to consider everything, a sense of humor and playfulness—qualities we are designed to develop rather than outgrow. Instead, we dismiss most of these traits by saying, "Don't be childish!"

Ashley Montague, Princeton University sociologist, says we should say instead, "Don't be adultish!" He says most of us have been victims of a conspiracy against learning not only how to grow older, but also how to grow *up*. He says most older people play the role of being old, one of the most serious diseases of modern times—what Dr. Montague calls *psychosclerosis*: hardening of the mind. People need to listen to the "Promethean voice," the call of the upward pull of the divine within. While the aging process says, "Why don't you grow up?" the youthing process says, "Why don't you grow onward? The best is yet to be."

Growing old takes no effort and is usually accompanied by the attitude that life just happens and you can do nothing about it. But growing *onward* takes effort and discipline to keep interested and interesting, enthusiastic and involved. André Maurois says that aging is no more than a bad mental habit which a busy person has no time to acquire.

Wherever you are on the human scale of measuring life by years, you are alive, and thus you are a full-fledged member of a dynamic Universe. So when and if retirement comes, it is important to make a new commitment to go into *entirement*—to remember that you are a whole person, and that wholeness is not fragmented by retirement, except in your own attitude.

The problem of retirement is not that employers coldly turn people out of jobs, or that benefits do not keep pace with inflation or the cost of living, even though these matters are important. The major tragedy of retirement is the common perception of being supported to go off and do nothing. This attitude is extremely aging. An exhaustive sociological study made of centenarians (people living beyond age 100) turned up the interesting fact that keeping busy was one thing they all had in common. Not one retired-to-do-nothing person was found in this group.

In the plan for your *en*tirement there must be a commitment never to retire in the sense of resignation from a life of creativity and usefulness. Never get boxed into a position where you are "out of it." The sense of remaining "in" can be acquired in many ways. You may not be able to find "gainful employment," but there is much to be gained in willingly doing useful, helpful things.

Gerald Heard says that retirement should be a time when the person can devote himself to the full reaping of his potentialities. Unless we seriously get involved in the full reaping of our potentialities, the word *retirement* may become a stigma. There is a life-change involved, and we need to have a positive attitude toward the change. How much better to continue the process of growth through education or travel or some kind of volunteer service than to take part in some passive activity!

Without some activity, there is the likelihood that one will begin to experience fatigue and apathy. A well-to-do society matron had a deep-seated fatigue that made her very bones ache. Her doctor told her that she should get a job of some kind. She protested, "But doctor, I am so utterly tired all the time, I can hardly get through the day." He replied, "My dear woman, what you need is something to be tired *from*, not tired *of*." It is boredom that causes life to lose its meaning, and the psychological stage is set for all sorts of organic and debilitating diseases.

Of course, having employment does not of itself give you a sense of meaning in life. So often people mistakenly say, "I wish I had a job with meaning." But *no* job has meaning. *People* have meaning, and they do their work meaningfully. They invest meaning in their work. As Emerson said, "Let your work be organic, let it be in your bones." In other words, live wholly; "Work out your life no longer by halves, but in all its beauty and totality."

A common problem in the feeling of emptiness and the lack of meaning in work is the perception of "making a living," instead of *making a life*—the idea that working for pay is the sole meaning of life. Your work is an opportunity to give expression to your creative ability. When you go into *entirement*, you have the feeling of giving yourself away. This feeling of giving not only brings a sense of meaning, but it is the key to receiving the rewards and the success of the world.

One of the reasons for so much unhappiness and frustration among people in today's world is that because of mass-media entertainment, people do not get enough involved in individual creative effort. For the most part, we have our creative experiences vicariously. Athletically inclined people watch sports instead of participating in some athletic activity. Musically inclined people listen to great music but do not play or sing themselves. We read but we do not write. We appreciate art, but we do not paint. We watch great construction projects as "sidewalk superintendents," but we do not build homes or rooms or even footstools. People say that they plan one day to write a book. But with all the self-improvement means available, it could be said that the difference between a writer and a would-be writer is procrastination.

Get the sense of *en*tirement, the realization that you are a whole expression of a whole Universe. The whole of God is present in you as your potential for a full, meaningful, creative, and fully functioning life. We have erroneously thought that a waning interest in goals and new developments, and a resistance to change, are symptoms of age. Actually, it might better be said that they are *causes* of aging. The person who keeps himself alive in mind and heart keeps himself alive in body, regardless of the passing years.

Show me a person who has experienced apathy and depression in retirement, and I will show you many others who have retained security, serenity, cheerfulness, optimism, and enthusiasm for life. Such persons have gone into *retirement* in their later years, but they went into *en*tirement early in life. Thus they prepared themselves with diverse, broad goals and interests. They were not limited to their employment to give their life meaning. While they live, they are alive. Life flows in them unchecked, unhampered, unrestricted, and they are as vigorous, as expanding, as full of interior growth in the years of their maturity as many people are in adolescence.

Retirement for many persons is the beginning of the end. Get the idea that *it is just the end of the beginning*. As Browning puts it: "the last of life for which the first was made."

Sir Christopher Wren, who has become famous for building the magnificent St. Paul's Cathedral in London, did it in a post-retirement career. He had been a professor of astronomy at Gresham College, Oxford. After retirement, he became an architect. In the next forty years this amazing man built fifty-three churches and cathedrals, most of which stand today as monuments to his greatness. It is obvious he had gone into *en*tirement early in life and thus was prepared for retirement as a simple transition to a continuing experience of full and creative living.

No matter where you are in life on the scale of years, make the decision to go into *en*tirement. Get a sense of the wholeness of life. Resolve to keep open in mind and spirit to the upward progressive sweep of abundant life. Keep the capacity for wonder. Keep putting yourself in touch with new things.

Life is dynamic, not static. People who cannot change cannot grow. We have been conditioned to believe that following rituals is a sign of aging. It is important now to admit that it is more a *cause* of aging. Take a personal inventory of your life. Where you find yourself slavishly following patterns of sameness, you are aging. Start *youthing*. Reach eagerly for the new, the exciting, and the different. Your very life may depend on it.

What is most important: when you are in *entire*ment, it is not a question of age. Life is an experience of growth, a process of development and unfoldment. Thus at forty a person should be twice as well equipped to receive and use the blessings of life as at twenty. At sixty he should be three times as equipped; at eighty, four times. Knowing this—really knowing this—will not only add years to your life; it will add life to your years.

In *entire*ment, you will never retire, in the sense of retreating from life. You will always consciously be a vital part of a creative Universe, alive and healthfully living in it, and lavishly supported by it. And, like Goethe, you will always "work out life not by halves, but in all its beauty and totality."

PosiTrend:

I resolve to stay alive
as long as I live.

I will keep open in mind and spirit
to the upward progressive sweep
of abundant life.

I am a vital part
of a creative Universe
alive and healthfully living in it
and lavishly supported by it.

In a youthful spirit
I reach eagerly for the new
the exciting and the different
as if my life depended on it
which it does.

➤ At the close of the twentieth century, most persons could be described as "in drift." Aimlessness and lack of meaning are common. Without a sense of direction there can be no meaning, and without meaning life is only half lived. Heard often are cries such as "What's it all about?" And "Where are we going?" As with a meandering sailboat, we need to take the helm and set a constructive course. You can do what you want to do and be what you want to be—if you take charge of your life.

11

Quo Vadis?

In most of the twentieth century, at least in the Western World, people have had a strange fascination with the future. In fiction and in the comics we have described cities of the future and space travel in the year 2000; and in the last decade of the twentieth century, we have had our own world of hi-tech and computers on line, as well as the electronic superhighway. We have seen so many fabulous changes in just one lifetime that we look forward with almost breathless anticipation, wondering "What's next?" Quo Vadis?

That is the rough translation of the Latin, *quo vadis*. Some of you will remember it as the name of a classic motion picture of five decades ago, from the book *Quo Vadis* (1950), by Henryk Sienkiewicz. It was a dramatization of a story that continually asks the question "Where are we going?"

Humankind seems to have this forward-looking approach to all things—except in the case of religion. Religions traditionally look backward to other times. We are urged to remember "the day when God walked the earth," to find help and inspiration in the prophets of old. The tendency in religion is to "worship in retrospect."

Then, when religion does look to the future, it looks to the Millennium with its prophesied Battle of Armageddon, an end-of-the-world scenario in which Jesus is called into God's Kingdom, taking with him those who have qualified by being "Saved," with the rest relegated into a Hell of fire.

Could it be that that one reason for the imbalance in the world, giving rise to wars and all manner of man's inhumanity to man, is that while humankind makes steady progress in knowledge of the universe around them, they accept the dogmatic assertions that imply knowledge of the world within them stopped at some time in the revered past? While science and education are continually evolving, progress in religion comes slowly, if at all.

This statement shocks many traditionalists, who remark, "How can we progress beyond God's word, beyond the eternal creeds and the great historic Truths?" Certainly if there is one sure thing, it is that Truth cannot be changed. But Truth is an ultimate, beyond conscious knowing or verbalizing. All that persons have ever had, or have today, are insights into Truth, which must be subject to continued inspiration and expansion.

As we have said, the year 2000 will not automatically bring dramatic change. It is a metaphor for the opportunity of change. If contemporary religions avail themselves of the millennial opportunity, they will evolve a millennial theology in which religion will not be centered in churches, but in *living*. It will not be a way of worship, but a way of *life*. Its purpose will not be to create great congregations, but to produce *enlightened people*. When we have enlightened people at the bargaining table, enlightened people in the councils of government, enlightened people as teachers, officials, and parents, then the problems of society will easily be resolved.

Religious institutions will be laboratories for the study and practice of the reality of creative love. We will realize, with the same sort of seriousness with which we deal with nuclear fission, that the absence of love between persons or nations can destroy the world. We will be conditioned to a universal law of love, much in the way we were taught to obey the civil law. This law will articulate the principle that maintaining the flow of mutuality and love is everybody's business.

One of the greatest visions for the future of the race ever uttered is found in the words of Robert Browning:

> Progress is
> The law of life, man is not Man as yet.
> Nor shall I deem his object served, his end
> Attained, his genuine strength put fairly forth,
> While only here and there a star dispels
> The darkness, here and there a towering mind
> O'erlooks its prostrate fellows. When the host
> Is out at once to the despair of night,
> When all mankind alike is perfected,
> Equal in full-blown powers—then, not till then,
> I say, begins man's general infancy.

During the past century we have made unbeliev-
able progress in understanding and developing the
resources of the world we live in. But it is probably
true that we have been more successful in exploring
the depths of the material universe than in plumbing
the spiritual depths of ourselves. Now is the time to
get seriously involved in what Christopher Fry calls
"an adventure into God." Man must begin to see himself as an integral part of a whole Universe rather
than simply a lonely inhabitant of a small planet in
a vast and indifferent cosmos.

With our highly sophisticated technological equipment we are in instant contact with all parts of the
world; but we still have difficulty communicating
with each other. We watched while the astronauts
circled the moon and made their lunar landing—but
we are strangely blind to the needs of our ghettos.
It may well be that we needed a "space" viewpoint
of ourselves and our society. Perhaps the most sig-

nificant moment of all history, to date, was when we were able to look back to earth and see the "blue planet" for the first time from a moon perspective.

In a subtle but deeply profound way, this new world-view may influence the development of what Lancelot Whyte calls Unitary Man. He feels that we have been trying to understand our material life and a mechanical universe without an adequate rule of measurement. It has been partial man, in partial self-understanding, trying to cope with a partial universe. Unitary man will begin to deal with himself as a whole person and not just a disembodied spirit. In the consciousness of unity, he will deal easily with all kinds of people and with groups and nations.

Thomas Mann: "Time has no divisions to mark its passage. There is never a thunderstorm or blare of trumpets to announce the beginning of a new month or a new year. Even when a new century begins, it is only we mortals who ring bells and fire off pistols."

A religious zealot once came to Emerson with the grim news: "The world is coming to an end." Emerson tartly replied, "I can get along without it."

A human's earliest interest in religion, or in God, or in providence, springs from the desire to see forward (which is the literal meaning of providence). Christianity was intended to be a prophetic religion and way of life. Jesus is not much more than a figure in history if he comes to life only as we look backward. He is and must always be a promise of the ultimate of all of us.

One of the confusions arising from dealing with

futurism concerns what is called "The Divine Plan." Shakespeare says, "There is a divinity that shapes our ends, rough-hew them how we will." It has a good ring to it, doesn't it? But wait a minute! Does it mean you might as well accept things as they come, that you can't escape your destiny? That God's will for you is fixed? That is predestination.

Do you accept this—that your whole future is all laid out for you? If everything is foreordained for you, then what good does it do to pray for any change of events or circumstances?

Yet we cannot deny the phenomenon of prophecy. Every person has a latent extra-sense that leads at times to an intuitive awareness of events to come. Question: "Does the forecaster or prophet foresee what is predestined to occur? Or is it a sensing of states of consciousness that indicate a tendency toward certain ends?" In other words, are we dealing with predestination or *predisposition*? The prophetic insight simply reads patterns of thought (William James calls it "streams of consciousness")—not that which will happen, but that which seems likely to happen if the pattern or stream of thought continues on its present course.

If, from some lofty perch, you see two trains on the same track, speeding around a blind corner toward one another, you could easily forecast an impending collision. But note that someone could flag the trains and thus avert the inevitable. The fact that prophecy is sometimes accurate seems to indicate that human nature is inclined to move in ruts, to resist change.

At a certain rural crossroads in Canada, on a dirt road where the spring thaw makes travel almost impossible, there is a sign nailed on a tree that reads, "Take care which rut you choose: you may be in it for the next 20 miles."

A great misconception about the Bible prophets is that they were "crystal-gazers." They sensed a coming of chaos, but they preached a change of consciousness. Their constant theme was "Repent." We have mistakenly thought that they were grimly saying, "Make your peace with God, for the end is near. You want to be sure to get accepted for heaven, or else you will burn in hell through all eternity."

But *repent* means "change your mind." The prophets sensed a strong predisposition toward a certain result, but they believed that the tragedy could be forestalled if there were a change of consciousness. What seemed like the beginning of the end could be the end of the beginning. We can flag the train, get centered on the right track, and go forward to a new era of unfoldment.

The Bible does speak of a form of predestination: "For whom he did foreknow, he also did predestinate to be conformed to the image of his Son" (Romans 8:29). This means that the ultimate goal of every life is set. Each of us is created in the image-likeness of God. And it is ordained that we will ultimately manifest in the outer that image-likeness. But the human destiny, the way of attainment, the path we take in achieving this goal is completely shaped by our thoughts and actions, our ideals and aspirations, our reactions to the everyday experiences that confront us.

Meanwhile we have certain clear-cut predispositions that spell the roads best suited to us. However, though the choice of human experience is always with us, and though we do make what seem to be mistakes that bring inharmony and even chaos, yet we can never lose that divine catalyst of Spirit which forever works to bring plan and purpose out of all discord. I call it the "divine law of adjustment," by which even the "goof," like the accidental dissonance of the pianist, may be resolved into a beautiful progression of harmony, and "all things work together for good."

You may look back in time and see how some horrible mistake has become a blessing. It might appear that it was planned that we go through that experience. But it was not predestined. As you look forward, you can actually forecast your future by decreeing your good. You can start a positive stream of consciousness, or *positrend*, which will literally be a "self-fulfilling prophecy."

The important meaning of the future for each of us lies in the continuing opportunity it provides for becoming what we can be. But we can't sit back and wait for it to happen out there in the tomorrow before us. The future is now! It is predestined that you will ultimately achieve the fulfilling of your Christ potential—but you must get busy creating the predisposition by which it can come.

On Times Square a religious zealot carried a sign: "Repent, The End Is Near." You may recall that song that was sung with such fervor by the "beautiful people" in the sixties: "The world ain't coming to an end, my friend; the world's just coming to a start."

In this book we have considered some ways in which we can prepare for the Millennium. We have focused on trends, prevailing tendencies, and patterns of mind that cry out for change; and we have considered how we can make simple changes in our way of life and also become change-agents in our world. We have labeled the areas where growth is needed as *negatrends*.

The most significant statement in the Bible is the lovely Shema, "Hear, O Israel, the Lord our God is One."

This does not refer to one thing or one person. It means *Whole*, but a whole that is present in fullness at every point in space at the same time. John says, "In the beginning was the word, and the word was with God, and the word was God." "Word" is from the Greek *Logos* (which in Greek philosophy is the "rational principle that governs and develops the Universe"). Theologians talk about "God's word," referring to the scriptures. But John's *Logos* is much more than that. It is not information (and inspiration) that is found in the Bible. It is the Divine Mind field from which the Bible is outformed—but also from which all information is outformed.

There is a sense in which the Universe is an unfinished symphony in the process of being composed, and as you compose yourself at the still point within,

you outform your own "song of life," which sings itself as you. When you experience limitation of any
kind, it indicates that you are not in tune with the
symphony of life. Quiet times should be a quest for
your song—not seeking to create it, but to discover
it. It is the song of your divinity.

In our metaphor your song is the Truth, and to sing
your song is to speak the word of Truth: to project
into your world of mind, body, and affairs the consciousness of spiritual Principle. To sing your song
is to synchronize yourself with healing life, inexhaust-
ible substance, and the radiance of love in all relationships. It is to tune in on a vital energy that is a
protecting force. Victor Hugo says, "Be like the bird
that rests on boughs too slight, and feels them give
way, yet sings, knowing that she has wings."

There is a beautiful oriental adage that says, "If
you keep in your heart a green bough, I have heard
. . . there will come . . . one day . . . to stay . . . a
singing bird." If you are centered on the green bough
of expectancy, there will come to stay a singing bird
of health or the vision of health; of overcoming or the
strength to overcome; of affluence or the attracting
power of substance; of love or the confidence of loving change.

There is a transcendent energy in the song of the
Universe. Like faith, it can move mountains and dissolve barriers. Paul and Silas were imprisoned and
shackled in irons. Scripture records that at midnight
they were praying and singing hymns, and suddenly
there was a great earthquake that shook the founda-

tions of the prison. The shackles fell off the prisoners, and the doors were opened. In personal symbolism this episode demonstrates the power of the song of your soul to set you free from all kinds of human bondage.

Remember the song "Singing in the Rain"? Who could forget the scene in the movie where Gene Kelly does that fabulous dance in the rain? Rain is a common occurrence in most lives. As the saying goes, "Into each life some rain must fall." To have a fully functioning life, one must learn to sing in spite of the rain. Jesus said, "In the world you have tribulation; but I have overcome the world." He was saying that although there may be problems in the Millennium, you can rise above them by keeping your consciousness on a higher level. You can be joyous and positive and at the same time be effective.

I have a feeling that Eugene O'Neill had heard the song of the soul, for in his play *Lazarus Laughed* he has Lazarus saying, "Why are your eyes fixed on the ground in weariness of thought or watching one another in suspicion? Throw your gaze upward to eternal life, to the fearless and the deathless, the everlasting, to the stars. . . . O brothers in God, weaving dance rhythms of eternal peace to the lonely drum of time, launch thine everlasting song, let it descend on man's seared lips. O brothers, sons of eternal life, celebrants of its flaming revel along the mountain ridges of infinity, let man feel thy ecstasy that he may evoke his own high freedom."

Yes, throw your gaze upwards! Give thanks for the

dramatic changes that are taking place throughout the world. The Third Millennium is already with us. It is the gateway into the Golden Age of life on the planet. True, there are great and powerful crosscurrents in our society, but thus it has always been for the human race and the world. We are growing, developing, and improving. Nietszche is purported to have said, "Man must have chaos in him to give birth to a dancing star."

The song of your soul reaches out and touches all persons everywhere. When you are singing your song of oneness, you will keep yourself in perfect peace even when the world seems to be falling down around you. But most importantly, you will become a vital part of an activity leading toward a peaceful state of the world. When Edward Bok established a bird sanctuary, building the pink marble "singing tower" in Florida, he imported nightingales from England. But it was not to be, for the nightingales became ill and died. Their exquisite music seemed lost forever. Then, to the astonishment of everyone, the song was heard again. For the mockingbirds had learned the song and were singing the song every bit as beautifully as the nightingales!

Every person has his own song. It is one's contribution to life. This song you sing is yours. It is you. The song will be heard, and repeated again by others, at least in part. I am sure we have all consciously or unconsciously learned to sing the songs of others. Many of the things we do are things we admired in someone else, and as a stage in our growth this is good. But though the song you sing is a reflection of the song of a respected teacher or guru, you can never be a fully functioning person until you find your own song and sing it with commitment.

Jesus favored the metaphor of light. "I am the light of the world. . . . you are the light of the world. Let your light shine." The vibration we call light is akin to the vibration we call music. Each person must light his own candle, and sing his own song. Light is everywhere, only sometimes we do not have the perception to see it. The sounds of music are everywhere, even if, as Carlyle put it, they are but "little dew drops of celestial harmony."

Somewhere a poet has said, "All things respond to the call of rejoicing, all things gather where life is a song." Your life is never quite complete, and your existence never fully justified until you know who you are, and you add the song of the soul of you to the cosmic symphony of life.

Quo Vadis? Actually, we are not going anywhere. The dateline that separates the Second and Third millennia is imaginary. The time is now! The year 2000 is not some country to migrate to. It is a potentiality to release. And it will be to you what you can conceive and believe.

According to our fantasy scenario, the Millennium is a universal consciousness, which we can experience every day. We want to see the ball of light as a "circle of light" encircling the totality of our life and affairs.

PosiTrend:

In the New Millennium
we affirm the principle
of the creation:
"Let there be."

"Let there be liberty
justice and righteousness
in all the affairs of the people
and the nations of Planet Earth.

Let there be respect
for the divinity within people
establishing love and brotherhood
in all relationships.

Let there be light
revealing a transcendent purpose
for existence.

Let there be an ever-expanding
knowledge of the Truth
that sets us free.

Let there be peace on earth
and let it begin with me."